Free Lover

Free Lover

Sex, Marriage and Eugenics
In the Early Speeches of
Victoria Woodhull

*And the Truth will Make You Free. A Speech
on the Principles of Social Freedom*

The Scare-crows of Sexual Slavery

The Elixir of Life

*Tried as by Fire; or The True
and the False Socially*

by

Victoria Woodhull

Introduction by Michael W. Perry

Inkling Books   Seattle   2005

Description

This book contains complete facsimile reproductions of the original editions of four speeches on free love published as pamphlets by Victoria C. Woodhull in 1873 and 1874. They are arranged in the chronological order of the speeches on which they are based. There is also an introductory chapter to provide background and introductions to each book by Michael W. Perry. The introductory chapter includes facsimiles of letters to the *New York Times* written in 1871 by Victoria Woodhull and a facsimile of an article in that paper about a speech she gave at Steinway Hall in 1872.

Publisher's Note

"Get Thee Behind me, (Mrs.) Satan!" The front cover art is from *Harper's Weekly*, 16:790 (Feb. 17, 1872), 140. The artist was Thomas Nast (1840-1902), considered by many to be the father of political cartooning. In the original wood engraving, the woman is saying, "I'd rather travel the hardest path of matrimony than follow your footsteps." Library of Congress Digital ID: cph 3b22237.

The Principles of Social Freedom (sometimes referenced as *And the Truth Shall Make You Free* or *A Speech on the Principles of Social Freedom*) was published in New York in 1874 by Woodhull & Caflin, Publ. It is based two speeches, one delivered at Steinway Hall, New York City on Monday, November 20, 1871 and the other at Music Hall in Boston on Wednesday, January 3, 1872.

The Scare-crows of Sexual Slavery: An Oration was published in 1874 by Woodhull & Caflin, Publ., New York, based on a speech given to 15,000 Spiritualists at Silver Lake, MA on Sunday, August 17, 1873.

The Elixir of Life or Why Do We Die? An Oration was published in 1873 by Woodhull & Caflin, New York. It is based on a speech given to the tenth annual convention of the American Association of Spiritualists at Grow's Opera House in Chicago on Friday, September 12, 1873.

Tried as by Fire; or, The True and the False Socially was published in 1874 by Woodhull & Caflin, New York. It is based on a speech given over "one hundred and fifty consecutive nights" in late 1873 and early 1874. The author claimed her total audience numbered "a quarter of a million of people."

With special thanks to: Special Collections at Southern Illinois University, Harvard University, Boston University, Yale University, University of Washington, New York Public Library, King County (Washington) Library System, Seattle Public Library, and Mary Shearer of VictoriaWoodhull.com.

Library Cataloging Data

Free Lover: Sex, Marriage and Eugenics in the Early Speeches of Victoria Woodhull

Victoria C. Woodhull (1837–1927) with introductions by Michael W. Perry (1948–)

Other published names include Victoria Woodhull Martin and Mrs. John Biddulph Martin.

Includes in facsimile all the texts of the four previously published pamphlets listed above.

183 pages, Size: 6x9 in, 229x152 mm Thickness: 0.42 in, 11 mm (pb) or 0.56 in, 14 mm (hb)

Library of Congress Control Number: 2005936210

ISBN-10: 1-58742-050-3   ISBN-13: 978-1-58742-050-4 (alkaline paperback)

ISBN-10: 1-58742-051-1   ISBN-13: 978-1-58742-051-1 (alkaline hardback)

ISBN-10: 1-58742-052-X   ISBN-13: 978-1-58742-052-8 (Adobe PDF ebook)

BISAC Subject Headings: HIS054000 HISTORY/Social History; HIS036040 HISTORY/United States/19th Century; SCI075000 SCIENCE/Philosophy & Social Aspects

Publisher Information

First edition, first printing, December 2005. Published in the United States of America on acid-free paper. Inkling Books, Seattle, WA, U.S.A. Internet: http://www.InklingBooks.com/

Contents

CHAPTER 1

"Yes, I am a Free Lover"

by Michael W. Perry

In early May of 1871, Victoria Woodhull's life seemed to be going marvelously. Under the patronage of Cornelius Vanderbilt, one of the nation's wealthiest men, her brokerage firm, Woodhull, Claflin & Company, was a financial success, providing the money for lavish parties where she met the most important people in New York City. She was also active politically. A year earlier, she began a newspaper, *Woodhull and Claflin's Weekly*, to promote herself as a candidate for President and to support voting "without distinction of sex."

Then disaster struck. On Monday, May 15 her mother Annie went to court, complaining that Woodhull's second husband, James Blood, had alienated her from her daughters and threatened, "not to go to bed until he had washed his hands in my blood." The trial was the talk of the town. In the end, there seemed to be little to the mother's charges beyond a fear she was inconvenient and might be sent to a "lunatic asylum" like Mrs. Vanderbilt.

But trials can spin out of control, particularly with a sensation-hungry press. From Blood's testimony, the public learned that Canning Woodhull, who was Woodhull's first husband, was living in the same house with her second husband, something that era found shocking and that even today might be regarded as odd. From the testimony of Tennie, Woodhull's sister, some picked up hints of sexual affairs in her claim that, "Many of the best men in [Wall] Street know my power. Commodore Vanderbilt knows my power." She meant her skill as a fortune teller, but it wasn't the wisest choice of words for an attractive woman to make, particularly since what was hinted was true. She was having an affair with the same Vanderbilt who had sent his wife to an insane asylum, so the mother's fears made sense.

The Beecher-Tilton Affair

As she often did, Woodhull decided that the best defense was to take the offensive. As Lois Underhill notes,[1] since the secrets of Woodhull's

---

1. Louis B. Underhill, *The Woman Who Ran for President: The Many Lives of Victoria Woodhull* (Binghampton: Bridge Works Pub., 1995), 179.

unconventional lifestyle would come out anyway, it was better to announce them herself and claim her behavior was based on principle. Saying nothing would lead the public to suspect she was driven by mere lust or (more likely) was using sex with powerful men to enrich herself

Woodhull made her first move in a pair of letters published in the *New York Times*. She issued a warning to the hypocrites among her critics, those who "preach against 'free love' openly, practice it secretly." In particular, she mentioned, "one man, a public teacher of eminence, who lives in concubinage with the wife of another public teacher of almost equal eminence." Some suspected the first was the popular liberal preacher of that generation, Henry Ward Beecher (1813–1887), pastor of the Plymouth Congregational Church in Brooklyn, New York. The second was thought to be Theodore Tilton (1835–1907), a member of his church and editor-in-chief of the influential *Independent*, a newspaper with as many as 500,000 readers.

In modern slang, Woodhull was 'coming out of the closet.' In her *Notorious Victoria*, Mary Gabriel notes that Woodhull had previously concealed her agreement with the radical ideas about marriage and sex being published in *Woodhull and Claflin's Weekly* by claiming she and her sister, "frequently differ widely from much which appears thus; … For ourselves we have no desire to state our convictions of truth."[2]

In the first letter, Woodhull remained vague. She limited herself to something easily defended—caring for her "sick, ailing" first husband in the home she shared with her second husband. She brought up free love only as something she advocated but not necessarily practiced, and only "in the highest and purest sense"—whatever that means. She also tried to divert attention from herself to those who secretly practiced free love while publicly denouncing it. In her second letter she also attacked differing sexual standards for men and women.

On the following three pages are Woodhull's 'coming out' letter from Saturday, May 20, 1871, reproduced exactly as it was published two days later on Monday, followed by an even angrier letter written on Tuesday, May 23 and published the following day.[3]

---

2. Mary Gabriel, *Notorious Victoria: The Life of Victoria Woodhull* (Chapel Hill: Alonquin Books, 1998), 64.
3. *New York Times*, May 22, 1871, p. 5 and May 24, 1871, p. 2.

Mrs. Woodhull and Her Critics.

To the Editor of the New-York Times :

Because I am a woman, and because I conscientiously hold opinions somewhat different from the self-elected orthodoxy which men find their profit in supporting; and because I think it my bounden duty and my absolute right to put forward my opinions and to advocate them with my whole strength, self-elected orthodoxy assails me, villifies me, and endeavors to cover my life with ridicule and dishonor. This has been particularly the case in reference to certain law proceedings into which I was recently drawn by the weakness of one very near relative and the profligate selfishness of other relatives.

One of the charges made against me is that I lived in the same house with my former husband, Dr. WOODHULL, and my present husband, Col. BLOOD. The fact is a fact. Dr. WOODHULL being sick, ailing and incapable of self-support, I felt it my duty to myself and to human nature that he should be cared for, although his incapacity was in no wise attributable to me. My present husband, Col. BLOOD, not only approves of this charity, but co-operates in it. I esteem it one of the most virtuous acts of my life. But various editors have stigmatized me as a living example of immorality and unchastity.

My opinions and principles are subjects of just criticism. I put myself before the public voluntarily. I know full well that the public will criticise me and my motives and actions, in their own way and at their own time. I accept the position. I except to no fair analysis and examination, even if the scalpel be a little merciless.

But let him who is without sin cast his stone. I do not intend to be made the scape-goat of sacrifice, to be offered up as a victim to society by those who cover over the foulness of their lives and the feculence of their thoughts with hypocritical mouth of fair professions, and by diverting public attention from their own iniquity and pointing the finger at me. I know that many of my self-appointed judges and critics are deeply tainted with the vices they condemn. I live in one house with one who was my husband; I live as the wife with one who is my husband. I believe in Spiritualism; I advocate free love in the highest, purest sense, as the only cure for the immorality, the deep damnation by which men corrupt and disfigure God's most holy institution of sexual relations. My judges preach against "free love" openly, practice it secretly. Their outward seeming is fair; inwardly they are full of "dead men's bones and all manner of uncleanness." For example, I know of one man, a public teacher of eminence, who lives in concubinage with the wife of another public teacher of almost equal eminence. All three concur in denouncing offenses against morality. "Hypocrisy is the tribute paid by vice to virtue." So be it. But I decline to stand up as "the frightful example." I shall make it my business to analyze some of these lines, and will take my chances in the matter of libel suits.

I have faith in critics, but I believe in public justice.   VICTORIA C. WOODHULL.

NEW-YORK, Saturday, May 20, 1871.

Mrs. Woodhull's Side of the Question.

To the Editor of the New-York Times:

The publication of my "Personal" in your paper of yesterday conformed with my previous opinion of your impartiality. I have no desire to further obtrude my personality on your columns. It is not of the individual woman but of the representative woman that I would now speak. In my person various editors and public speakers, of more or less weight, have chosen to attack principles on purely personal grounds. A well-known Joe Miller gives instance of a lawsuit in which there being no defense, the client's instructions were to blackguard the plaintiff's lawyer. This is precisely the disingenuous and cowardly line of practice in which I am the victim. Woman's suffrage and woman's rights being the issue and there being no defense, I am taken as the representative woman, and my personal character being maligned and depreciated, the cause suffers. Let it not be supposed that I assume to myself the character of representative. The assumption is on the part of those who, being anti-suffragists, can neither rise above prejudice nor meet the irrefragable justice of the woman's cause by honest argument. In this strait they blackguard the "plaintiff's lawyer."

I will not ask of you whether such a course is manly, is just. The editor of one of the leading journals of America cannot afford to defend such flagrant injustice. Through you I appeal to the public. But, in appealing to the public, I would carry my argument a little further. If I be a "notorious woman," a person with "soiled hands," and so forth, (I need not sully your columns with the filth and impurity of which I have been the target,) if I be all this, and thereby am rendered unfit to present and advocate the woman's cause, how is it with those—my opponents—who are themselves reprobate, and of impure life and conversation? I ask by what equity and justice a woman is to be held accused on the mere imputation of offenses which her accusers may commit without condemnation?

Let me ask a question of any one versed in public affairs. What man with sufficient ability and wealth to support a party is ever attacked on the score of his immorality or irreligion; in other words, for his drunkenness, blasphemy or licentiousness? These are his private life. To go behind a man's hall-door is mean, cowardly, unfair opposition. This is the polemical code of honor between men. Why is a woman to be treated differently? I claim as a matter of justice, by no means as of "gentle courtesy," that the same rule be observable toward the woman journalist or politician as toward the man.

This is natural equity; it is over and above the abuse of speech by lying and slanderous imputation.

I think you will acquit me of egotism in alluding to Woodhull & Claflin's Weekly; the same argument applies to the Weekly that applies to its editors. If the Weekly happen, in the exercise of its critical functions, to trench on the conduct or management of trading or corporate bodies, a howl resounds through the street, "Those women! those adventuresses! Black-mail!" If, without naming any one, notorious spots or blemishes are alluded to, whispers come round how Scrooze & Dickhoff intend to squelch those women, and drive them out of Broad-street. Let us see!

Woman suffrage will succeed, despite this miserable guerrilla opposition, and the Weekly is strong enough to take care of itself. But I only repeat: Is it fair to treat a woman worse than a man, and then revile her, because she is a woman?   VICTORIA C. WOODHULL.

NEW-YORK, Tuesday, May 23.

Woodhull's Steinway Hall Speech

Six months later, in a speech about "The Principles of Social Freedom" given on Monday, November 20, 1871 at Steinway Hall in New York City, Woodhull would make her opinion much clearer. As the date of the speech approached she appeared bold and defiant. A placard promoting it said her better known opponents were "specially invited to seats on the platform. All her lesser defamers should secure front seats."[4] Privately, Woodhull was terrified at standing on stage alone. Not only was what she would be saying controversial, she lived in the era before electronic sound systems. Her ability to be heard by several thousand people in a crowded auditorium depended on a cooperative audience. Anyone could shout as loudly as she could. A well-organized group could disrupt her speech and make her look foolish. Perhaps that was why she wanted her opponents to sit where they could be easily removed.

She hoped the nation's best known preacher, Henry Ward Beecher, would introduce her and give his stamp of approval. The allusion she made to a hypocritical "teacher of eminence" in her letter six months earlier (May 22) was a warning to him that his many sexual affairs would come out, and he should do as she had done. Privately, she tried to persuade him to go public with his behavior but failed. According to Woodhull, he said that if he appeared on that stage, "I should sink through the floor, I am a moral coward on the subject and I know it."

The New York Times covered her speech the next day (November 21, 1871) on its front page. The Mrs. Booker mentioned is Woodhull's younger sister, Utica. The question Utica hurled that evening is a telling criticism of free love: "How would you like to come into this world without knowing who your father and mother are?"[5] Woodhull's response, "There are thousands of noble men and women in the world today who never knew who their fathers were," missed her sister's point. Utica, whose troubles as a child still haunted her as an adult, would die the next year at thirty-one of alcoholism and drug abuse. She understood far better than her two stronger and more fortunate sisters how children need the stability of home, marriage and parents.

---

4. *Notorious Victoria,* 144.
5. *Notorious Victoria,* 147.

The difference between Utica's early death and the successful lives of Victoria and Tennie, illustrates the uneven impact the weakening or elimination of marriage that Woodhull advocated would have. With all her problems, Utica and any children she might have could become discards in a world of easy sex and quick divorce. Strong and ruthless, Victoria and Tennie could and did use those same circumstances to acquire membership in the British upper class, a option that by its very nature is open only to a tiny percentage of women.

Woodhull would get her revenge on Beecher in November of the following year (1872), after he failed to support her run for U.S. President, the first by a woman. She exposed his infidelities in a *Woodhull and Claflin* article timed to coincide with the celebration of Beecher's twenty-fifth year at Plymouth Church. Unfortunately, the Beecher affair that drew the most public attention was that with Theodore Tilton's wife, and it was Tilton who had been considerate enough to introduce Woodhull that night in place of Beecher.

At the bottom of this page and on the next is the (slightly mistitled) article from the Tuesday, November 21, 1872 issue of the *New York Times*. Notice the large audience she was able to assemble for the speech, which is republished here in Chapter 2. Woodhull certainly knew how to draw a crowd.

The Principle of Social Freedom, Involving Free Love, Marriage, Divorce, &c.—Lecture by Victoria C. Woodhull.

One of the largest audiences ever collected together in a public hall in this City assembled last night at Steinway Hall on the occasion of a lecture by Mrs. VICTORIA C. WOODHULL on " The Principle of Social Freedom, Involving Free Love, Marriage, Divorce, &c." The assemblage embraced representatives of all classes and conditions of social life, but the vast portion of it, it must be confessed, was undeniably composed of the curious and indifferent. The novelty of the doctrines enunciated, and the still greater novelty of their expression by a lady, excited the highest amount of curiosity, and though not wishing to interrupt the continuance of the lecture, the audience was twice compelled to condemn the theories advanced in loud and continued hissing. But the most peculiar feature in the evening's programme was the violent interruption of the lecturer by her own sister, Mrs. BROOKER, and her vehement denunciations of the principles advocated by Mrs. WOODHULL. That lady occupied the front box in the middle tier, on the right of the platform, and as she boldly stood to repudiate the sentiments of her sister, a perfect storm of cheers and counter-demonstrations greeted her appearance. For fully ten minutes the utmost confusion prevailed. Mrs. WOODHULL, in despair at being unable to continue her lecture, retired from the platform, and Mrs. BROOKER, still standing erect, demanded silence. A breach of order seemed imminent, and a Police officer was compelled to advance to the position occupied by Mrs. BROOKER and force her to resume her seat. Mrs. WOODHULL was then called to the platform, and continued her lecture to the close without further interruption. The chair was occupied by Mr. THEODORE TILTON, who, in introducing Mrs. WOODHULL, observed that, notwithstanding all insinuations to the contrary, she was a virtuous woman, and he could vouch for it. The lecture, which occupied two hours in its delivery, was directed chiefly to an attack on the marriage system, as at present constituted, as an outrage on individual freedom and a barrier to general happiness. She maintained that it should not partake more of the character of a contract than any other legal agreement, and that its continuance for a lifetime was preposterous and an outrage. On the question of marriage, as in all others which affected private life, the Government should not be permitted to interfere; and to suppose that they were virtuous because of the restraint which it imposes upon them was an insult to American women. She believed and gloried in free love which bound the parties to each other only during its existence, and severed their marital relations whenever either of the parties desired. The offspring of such love was best and purest. Mrs. WOODHULL here enumerated a host of distinguished personages whom she described as being born under such circumstances. She spoke at considerable length of the social evil, and sympathized with the unfortunate women while she condemned the men as infinitely more debased. In this connection she severely commented on marriage for position and social elevation as the worst of evils, and concluded her lecture by expressing her conviction of the final triumph of free love.

Thinking Clearly about Woodhull's Speeches

In the next chapter, we turn to one of Woodhull's early published speeches in favor of free love. Keep in mind that in her day many were angry at how then-strict laws about marriage and divorce sometimes treated men or women, and that many had trouble seeing that the problem was with the specifics of the law rather than with marriage itself. Also, the fact that Woodhull's claims were novel appealed to those who are drawn to new things, just as surely as they outraged those who want things to stay the same. Neither group is necessarily right.

Today the situation is reversed. Divorce is so easy, eliminating it might seem a small step. In practice, marriage is not being eliminated. But it is being watered down to mean no more than a 'significant' relationship with anyone of either sex, a relationship with appealing tax and medical benefits. At that point, today's radical might ask why marriage should be limited to one or, stressing the 'significant,' if someone could marry a pet or the thing (perhaps a car) that matters most to them. Woodhull's once radical arguments are now so commonplace, they are either self-evident truths that must imposed on the unwilling, typically by court dictate, or they are an irresponsible folly that's more absurd and cruel than the strict nineteenth-century laws Woodhull attacked so long ago.

To better understand Woodhull, we need to step back and think carefully about what she was saying, asking how a society built as she suggested would actually work. The rest of this chapter offers examples based on her speech, "The Principles of Social Freedom" (Chapter 2), but the approach works equally well with the other three.

Keep in mind that Woodhull later rejected what she said here. She even sued the British Library for having in its collection a rarely checked out book about her earlier life.[6] Of course, her change of heart came in no small part from a desire to marry Mr. John Biddulph Martin, an eminently respectable member of a prominent British banking family. Woodhull knew how to come out on top. But readers should ask whether the norms for sexual behavior and the laws for marriage should serve the interests of those as attractive, clever and ruthless as she undoubtedly was, or whether they should serve everyone, paying particular attention to the weak, such as her sister, the unfortunate Utica Brooker.

---

6. See the *Times* (London) for Wednesday, January 24, 1894, page 3.

1. Living in a Different Era

It has been said by a very wise person that there is a trinity in all things…
(Page 3 in the original text)

When we read something old, we should remember it really is old, that its writer and readers lived in a different world from our own. Woodhull knew many in her audience were skeptical about what she was saying, so she started with something widely accepted by those educated in the nineteenth century. In her first three paragraphs she built on the then-common belief that the universe is so orderly that "all things" come in threes. If you accept the importance of two freedoms: religious and political, Woodhull was telling her readers, you must accept my third or social freedom. To modern readers that sounds absurd. If taken as true, this rule of three would mean that we can't add a fourth freedom, economic, or a fifth, artistic. "Things don't necessarily come in threes," we would rightly say. But while laughing at quirks in the beliefs of those long ago, we should not forget that we have our own quirks. Today appeals to self and personal choice are often carried to extremes as absurd as Woodhull's rule of three. They put too much emphasis on the rule of three, while we put too much emphasis on the rule of one. Personal freedom has to be balanced with personal responsibility.

2. Going to Extremes

If a person govern, not only himself but others, that is despotic government… (4)

Woodhull was a brilliant debater, and to persuade others she often portrayed a minor problem as a great evil. Are we living in a "despotic government" if some official requires us to sort our garbage or not park our car for more than two hours on a certain street? No, a despotic government isn't one that makes rules. All governments do that. A despotic government is one that is answerable to no one but itself.

How can we reconcile that remark with her own political agenda, stated under "Prospectus" two pages earlier? The first item doesn't say that everyone can participate in her new government, it says they *will*. Rather scary. The second seems to hint at land confiscation. The third, if it makes any sense at all, suggests that someone could not work in a factory without taking on the hassles of management, yet more forced participation. The fourth denies to buyer and seller the right to set their own prices, which suggests Woodhull was hostile to economic freedom. The fifth means our only choice of a bank would be a government one. The sixth is what she was advocating in this speech. The seventh has the government determine how "all children" are educated, taking that decision away from parents. In short, Woodhull's own agenda was far more despotic than anything in nineteenth-century America. The fact that she may have been getting those ideas from shadowy advisors, as some suggest, does not excuse her for promoting them.

Most maddening of all were her inconsistencies. As the head of a brokerage house when such businesses were also quasi-banks, She was violating at least three of her own principles and getting rich doing so.

3. Muddled Ideas about Rights

And the most perfect exercise of such rights is only attained when every individual is not only fully protected in his rights but also strictly restrained to the exercise of them within his own sphere and positively prevented from proceeding beyond its limits ... (7)

To a limited extent, what Woodhull was saying makes sense. Each of us has a right to our religious beliefs and no right to impose them on others. Each of us also has a right to vote, but no right to prevent others from voting or to force them to vote in a particular way. But remember that she wants to extend these easily reconciled religious and political freedoms into the social arena, particularly to marriage and sex where things are more complex and where what one person does invariably affects others. In those cases, rights always have winners and losers, so any talk of "his own sphere" is useless. Marriage lies not only within the "sphere" of a husband and a wife, it's within the sphere of their children, their parents, and even their community and nation as a whole.

Look at the conflicts complete sexual freedom entails. Can a wealthy businessman such as Cornelius Vanderbilt reward mistresses with business favors? If that's his right, can his wife be "positively prevented" from protesting by sending her to an asylum? Can those owning stock in his corporations complain when his favors to mistresses reduce dividends? And how do you deal with the children, in or out of wedlock, who result from these liaisons? If you eliminate legal marriage, as

Woodhull suggested, will the children of a long-term relationship inherit more than those born from a single night's affair?

It seems clear that Woodhull's either-or rights scheme has problems, particularly when a rights-based solution to every conflict is extended into personal relationships where the cost of one person's 'right' over another can be extremely high. But it gets even messier.

4. Misapplying Rights

I have before said that every person has the right to, and can determine for himself what he will do, even to the taking of the life of another … If the person succeed in taking the life, he thereby demonstrates that he is a tyrant who is at all times liable to invade the right to life, and that every person in the community is put in jeopardy by the freedom of this person. Hence it is the duty of the government to so restrict the freedom of this person to make it impossible for him to ever again practice such tyranny. (9)

Here Woodhull was opposing capital punishment, assuming a murderer retains an "inalienably vested" right to life. But does it make sense to act as if a first murder is wrong only because the murderer (confused with a tyrant) might commit a second, or that he is then automatically a threat to "every person in the community?" Left with her ill-acquired wealth, a wife who poisoned a rich husband would probably not pose a threat to anyone else. Why treat her as if she was? And why have such a strong regard for a potential second's victim's right to life, but so little for the person who was actually murdered?

What Woodhull wrote in the next paragraph was even odder. If someone steals, as with murder we are to prevent him from ever doing it again. But that can only be accomplished by locking him up for the rest of his life, no worst punishment than she would give to the serial killer of a dozen people. That makes no sense.

5. Marriage Is Not a Business Contract

The logical deduction of the right of two people to make a contract without consulting the government, or any third party, is the right of either or both of the parties to withdraw without consulting any third party, either in reference to its enforcement or as to damages. (10)

Again Woodhull's logic was strange. The fact that the government plays little or no role in the making of a contract doesn't mean the government should not enforce contracts. Modern courts spend quite a bit of time doing just that. The government has little expertise in determining whether two businesses should sign a contract. But there are excellent reasons for it to enforce contracts and keep the ultimate power to enforce them in government hands. It keeps people from having to resort to Mafia-like enforcement techniques, and it makes the weak backed by the government the equal of the strong. Revealingly, here Woodhull showed a remarkable indifference to situations where the strong ride roughshod over the weak. She was, after all, a great friend of the era's infamous 'robber barons.'

Of course, Woodhull's real target wasn't business contracts. The stock market in which she worked depended on contracts being enforceable. She has another sort of contract in mind, the life-long contract of marriage. That's why on the following page she asks why "the social relations of the sexes" should be treated any differently from easily terminated business contracts. We can fire our plumber on a whim, she suggests, why can't we fire our spouse? Perhaps because marriage is more important than a leaky drain pipe.

6. The Radical's Fallacy

> *Over the sexual relations, marriages have endeavored to preserve away and to hold the people in subjection to what has been considered a standard of moral purity. Whether this has been successful or not may be determined from the fact that there are scores of thousands of women who are denominated prostitutes, and who are supported by hundreds of thousands of men... (12)*

Here Woodhull adopted the Radical's Fallacy. Since marriage has problems, she said, we must radically alter or eliminate it. The same could be said about her system or that of anyone else. All social systems have problems because people are part of them and people are inherently flawed. A better response is to correct or at least reduce the problems with marriage in sensible ways without adopting the greater evil of throwing it out altogether. Woodhull's later life certainly demonstrates that she recognized the value of a stable marriage when it benefited her. Why shouldn't other people be able to enjoy what she enjoyed?

7. Hinting at Eugenics

Now to what more than to anything else do humanity owe their welfare and happiness? Most clearly to being born into earthly existence with a sound and perfect physical, mental and moral beginning of life, with no taint or disease attaching to them, either mentally, morally or physically. (13)

To counter her opponents, Woodhull made strong claims about the benefits of free love. Although she did not use the word eugenics, which had yet to be coined, that was what she described. Like later eugenists, she claimed that social ills could be eliminated by giving every child an ideal beginning. Notice that she gave this speech to a large audience in November of 1871. Francis Galton, who is generally credited with founding the eugenic movement, did not take up the cause in earnest until 1901, thirty years later. That's why *Lady Eugenist* suggests that Woodhull has at least as much claim to be the pioneering eugenist as the far better known Francis Galton.

Woodhull did not tell her audience something that should be obvious on reflection—that her call for babies to be born "with a sound and perfect physical, mental and moral beginning" meant that a small cadre of scientific experts would decide who could have children. Her free love belief in a right to sex with anyone at any time did not extend to a corresponding right to have children from that sex. Never forget that. It's the only way free love can be linked to reducing social problems.

Note her "born into earthly existence." That hints at her Spiritualism, and may explain why her earliest ideas about eugenics differed from the scientific variety that would become fashionable among elite, educated, progressive, and wealthy groups in the early twentieth century. Judging by her later writings (see *Lady Eugenist*), over time Woodhull's own eugenics became less mystical and more scientific.

8. Creating a False Dichotomy

Marriage must consist of either love or of law, since it may exist in form with either term absent; that is to say, people may be married by law and love be lacking; and they may also be married by love and lack all sanction of law. True marriage must in reality consist entirely either of law or love, since there can be no compromise between the law of nature and statute law by which the former shall yield to the latter. (14)

Either-or arguments are intended to force people to make choices they need not make. The fact that some women in her day were forced into unhappy, unloving marriages of convenience does not mean that all marriages sanctioned by law are hostile to love. At this point, most will ask, "Why not both love and legal ties as the best of both worlds?"

In addition, replacing a legal institution like marriage with intangible feelings is fraught with difficulties. How can inheritance be based on whether Man A was in love with Woman B? How does B prove the now-dead A loved her, particularly if their relationship was secret? What if other women claim Man A loved only them and thus that they deserve his great fortune? The problem might be solved by eliminating inheritance and letting the government take everyone's estate on their death, but would it be good for the government to acquire small businesses or homes, and how effective would it be at looking after the widows and orphans it impoverished? Laws are linked. Changing one creates enormous complications with others.

9. Can Freedom Exist Without Self-control?

> *Two persons, a male and a female, meet and are drawn together by a mutual attraction—a natural attraction unconsciously arising within their natures of which neither has any control—which is denominated love. (17)*

This sentence lies at the heart of Woodhull's difficulties. People, she said, must be free to have sex unrestricted by law or social restrictions. But how can this sexual attraction be "free" when it is imposed by nature and where "neither has any control" over what happens? If nature forces people to feel a certain way, then society is merely being like nature when it forces those feelings to be properly channeled. Slaves of their natures and impulses, these "two persons" have no real freedom to be violated.

Our natural impulses also drive us to want to get rid of those we dislike and to possess things we don't own. That doesn't mean that society can't pass laws against murder or theft. Woodhull agreed and said that this very inability to control oneself provided enough justification for society to lock someone up for life. If that's true, then the harm from a love that's a mere passing lust certainly justifies restrictions on sexual freedom that fall well short of life imprisonment.

10. Selfishness Backed by Coercion

And to those who denounce me for this I reply: "Yes, I am a Free Lover. I have an inalienable, constitutional, and natural right to love whom I may, to love as long or as short a period as I can; to change that love every day if I please, and with that right neither you nor any law can frame any right to interfere. And I have the further right to demand a free and unrestricted exercise of that right, and it is your duty not only to accord it, but as a community, to see that I am protected in it. I trust that I am fully understood, for I mean just that, and nothing less! (23–24)

These two sentences were at the very heart of Woodhull's agenda in the early 1870s. They would also give her grief later in life when she wanted to become a respectable member of a British upper class that, however promiscuous some of its members might be in private, did not approve of those who flaunted that behavior in public.

It's easy to see why people reacted negatively. Can genuine love flip on and off as easily as she described? "I will love you from nine this evening until nine tomorrow morning," Woodhull was asserting, "but after that I don't care if I ever see you again." Her critics may be right when they claim she was simply using sex to advance herself.

The second sentence is even more disturbing. Neither individuals ("you") nor society ("any law") had "any right to interfere" with her behavior. Instead, she claimed individuals and the community have a "duty" to make sure no one hindered her behavior. In concrete terms, since the only thing most people can do about promiscuity is to call it wrong, if free love came in, free speech must exit. Criticizing those who practice it would be illegal. Here Woodhull was a pioneer. Similar arguments lie behind modern-day demands that those who criticize certain sexual behaviors should be prosecuted for "hate speech."

Perhaps that's why in 1894 Woodhull took the unusual step of suing the British Library for having in its collection a copy of book critical of her behavior during the early 1870s (see page 13). When she wanted to be promiscuous, it was to be illegal to criticize her. When she wanted to be respectable, the same was true. Woodhull might change the cause she was promoting, remaining steadfast and zealous only in her advocacy of eugenics, but she was never a genuine champion of freedom.

11. 'Paradise Regained' but Freedom Lost

… I believe in love with liberty; in protection without slavery; in the care and culture of offspring by new and better methods and without the tragedy of self-immolation on the part of the parents. I believe in the family, spiritually constituted, expanded, amplified, and scientifically and artistically organized, as a unity home. I believe in the most wonderful transformation of human society as about to come, as even now at the very door, through general progress, science, and the influential intervention of the spirit world.... and I believe that in order to prepare minds to contemplate and desire and enact the new and better life, it is necessary that the old and still prevalent superstitious veneration for the legal marriage tie be relaxed and weakened; not to pander to immorality, but as introductory to a nobler manhood and a more glorified womanhood; as indeed, the veritable gateway to a paradise regained. (42)

In this paragraph, the fourth from the last, Woodhull dropped hints about her broad social agenda. There's "love with liberty," her free love scheme with that most obvious of problems—can something that can be terminated at any time by either party against the wishes of the other ("liberty") really be "love," when it is, at best, a fleeting infatuation.

"Protection without slavery" was her plan to alter the economics of marriage. With proper training, most women, like most men, can support themselves. But when both marry and have children, the situation changes. The cost in time and money to raise children makes it difficult to do alone. Woodhull was rebelling against the common and practical division of labor between wife and husband, where he provides the bulk of the income, while she spends more time at child rearing. But it's no more slavery that she depends on him for money, than it's slavery for him to labor at a job he may hate and depend on her greater skills at child rearing. That's where egalitarianism often goes wrong. There's no inherent virtue in sameness, and differences between two people don't make one a slave and the other a master.

"Offspring," she went on, using a term more often used of animals, must be reared "by new and better methods." Here we draw close to her real agenda. Scientific organizers are to be supreme, unhindered by meddlesome parents, whose "tragedy of self-immolation" probably meant their fretting and worrying because child rearing has traditionally been their responsibility rather than a duty of the state. "The legal marriage tie," she is hinting, must be weakened in order to introduce a new sort of family. Bound by links no more lasting than passing fancy, there would be no real marriage to oppose "progress, science and the influential intervention of the spirit world."

The last refers to her Spiritualism (see Chapter 4), and that's probably what led her to call herself a "transcendental socialist" in the next paragraph. Today, when socialism is almost always secular and materialistic, it's easy to forget that it's possible to create an all-intrusive State grounded in a religion that has little regard for the marriage and family life of individuals. Religions that add a sacred character to marriage, such as historic Judaism and Christianity, often come under attack for resisting the weakening of marriage and the growing power of a scientifically organized State (see Chapter 3).[7] That's why G. K. Chesterton, a Catholic writer and the author of *Eugenics and Other Evils*, was one of the few intellectuals to criticize eugenics when it was at its strongest during the 1910s and 1920s.

Woodhull claimed her eugenic schemes would bring a "nobler manhood," a "glorified womanhood," and the "gateway to a paradise regained." In the fall of 1871, as she championed free love, Woodhull was laying a foundation for eugenics and a justification for government coercion (see Chapter 5 and all of *Lady Eugenist*). Paradise was to be bought at the price of the freedom of individuals to marry, form families, and rear children, or, viewed from another angle, with a counterfeit sexual freedom. In her Brave New World, much like that of Aldous Huxley's 1932 novel by that name, you can get all the sex you can attract, but you aren't free to be a genuine parent. The superficial fun may be yours, but the future belongs to Woodhull and those who think like her. That idea remains all too common today, although in a much more covert form.

---

7. Some Islamic traditions, however much they may call marriage important, do not create a lasting bond between one man and one woman, "forsaking all others." Polygamy and easy divorce for men are, in a rough sense, like Woodhull's free love applied to one sex with all the resulting cruelties imposed on the other. Also, the result is often not a personal bond strong enough to resist the encroachment of a all-powerful State, either modern and scientific or primitive and tribal. Like nature, politics abhors a vacuum. When the family is weak, you are likely to get rule either by a scientific, managerial elite or by warring tribal chieftains. Neither is good.

CHAPTER 2

The Principles of Social Freedom
Introduced by Michael W. Perry

Perhaps because the original title page was formatted like a leaflet promoting a speech, in library databases this pamphlet has several titles including: "And the Truth Shall Make You Free, A Speech on the Principles of Social Freedom," and "The Principles of Social Freedom." Here, we will use the latter. We discussed the events in Woodhull's life that led up to this speech in Chapter 1.[1]

The November 20, 1871 speech in New York City's Steinway Hall, which was published in this pamphlet, was rooted in the controversies of the American Association of Spiritualists (AAS). Two months earlier, Woodhull had been elected their president. Some AAS members were unhappy, suspecting, probably correctly, that she was using their organization to promote herself. Others disliked the controversial link she was establishing between spiritualism and free love. This speech was her defense against the latter group, as well as an attempt to deal with the growing controversy surrounding her beliefs.

Unfortunately for the later Woodhull, in this speech she took the radical position even among free lovers. Her claimed right to, "love whom I may, to love as long or as short a period as I can; to change that love every day if I please," (page 23 in the original), placed her within the "varietism" branch of the free lovers rather than the more conventional "serial monogamist" or "monogamist" points of view. Later she would claim that at this time she was under the influence of Stephen Pearl Andrews (1812–1886), her mentor and the author of an 1853 pamphlet, *Love, Marriage and Divorce*. Frisken explained the situation this way:

> Victoria's contemporaries interpreted this statement as a spontaneous response to audience heckling, and therefore an "authentic" reflection of her own views. In fact, it was likely the product of Andrew's thinking on individual sovereignty in sexual relations, and it appeared within the text of the speech itself, later sold in pamphlet form. Andrews took the "varietist" position that social freedom meant unconditional freedom from any restraints or

---

1. For the broader historical background see: Amanda Frisken, *Victoria Woodhull's Sexual Revolution* (Philadelphia : University of Pennsylvania Press, 2004), 37f.

conventions in intimate relations, whereas Woodhull's own views, to judge from her later statements, were probably closer to the serial monogamist position, at least in theory. She spent the next few years backpedaling from this extreme position on free love.[2]

Woodhull's claim that free love was the answer to the problems of women does not ring true. The "Mrs. Satan" graphic, created by the well-known cartoonist Thomas Nast and published in *Harper's Weekly* three months after Woodhull's speech, which is reproduced on the front cover, illustrates what many Americans thought of "Be Saved by Free Love." Frisken gets it wrong when she claims that Woodhull offered women an "easier path."[3] In most cases, even a far-from-perfect husband offers a woman more support, emotional and financial, than a frustrating series of lovers and one-night-stands. And while it may be a good idea to show a jerk the door, it's far more sensible not to let him in in the first place.

Woodhull's thinking on may have been influenced by odd utopians such as Stephen Paul Andrews, much as it was by her relationship with industrial barons whose great wealth could conceal a multitude of miseries inflicted on others. But anyone who has studied Woodhull's life will come away with a strong impression that, at least after she escaped the mistakes of her teen years and her disastrous first marriage, she was not the sort to be putty in anyone's hands. She is responsible for what she said and to treat her otherwise is to refuse to give her the respect that is her due.

Also, keep in mind that her core beliefs about the importance of eugenics and the role of government in imposing its agenda were remarkably consistent from these early 1870s speeches to her remarks, made two months before she died, in support of forced eugenic sterilization as expressed in the 1927 U.S. Supreme Court decision, *Buck v. Bell*. At that time the *New York Times* reported that she proudly claimed to have "advocated that fifty years ago."[4]

---

2. Amanda Frisken, *Victoria Woodhull's Sexual Revolution*, 40.

3. Amanda Frisken, *Victoria Woodhull's Sexual Revolution*, 48.

4. "Says Voting at 25 is 'Young Enough,'" *New York Times* (May 3, 1927) pt. 2, p. 6. See also *Lady Eugenist*, pages 9 and 56.

"And the Truth shall make you Free."

A SPEECH

ON

The Principles of Social Freedom,

DELIVERED IN

Steinway Hall, Monday, Nov. 20, 1871,

AND

Music Hall, Boston, Wednesday, Jan. 3, '72,

BY

VICTORIA C. WOODHULL,

To Audiences of 3,000 People in Each Place.

New York:
WOODHULL & CLAFLIN, PUBLISHERS.

1874.

PROSPECTUS.

WOODHULL & CLAFLIN'S WEEKLY.

[The only Paper in the World conducted, absolutely, upon the Principles of a Free Press.]

It advocates a new government in which the people will be their own legislators, and the officials the executors of their will.

It advocates, as parts of the new government—

1. A new political system in which all persons of adult age will participate.

2. A new land system in which every individual will be entitled to the free use of a proper proportion of the land.

3. A new industrial system, in which each individual will remain possessed of all his or her productions.

4. A new commercial system in which "cost," instead of "demand and supply," will determine the price of everything and abolish the system of profit-making.

5. A new financial system, in which the government will be the source, custodian and transmitter of all money, and in which usury will have no place.

6. A new sexual system, in which mutual consent, entirely free from money or any inducement other than love, shall be the governing law, individuals being left to make their own regulations; and in which society, when the individual shall fail, shall be responsible for the proper rearing of children.

7. A new educational system, in which all children born shall have the same advantages of physical, industrial, mental and moral culture, and thus be equally prepared at maturity to enter upon active, responsible and useful lives.

All of which will constitute the various parts of a new social order, in which all the human rights of the individual will be associated to form the harmonious organization of the peoples into the grand human family, of which every person in the world will be a member.

Criticism and objections specially invited.

The WEEKLY is issued every Saturday.

Subscription price, $3 per year; $1.50 six months; or 10c. single copy, to be had of any Newsdealer in the world, who can order it from the following General Agents:

The American News Co., New York City;

The New York News Co., New York City;

The National News Co., New York City;

The New England News Co., Boston, Mass.;

The Central News Co., Philadelphia, Pa.;

The Western News Co., Chicago, Ill.

Sample copies, mailed on application, free.

VICTORIA C. WOODHULL AND TENNIE C. CLAFLIN, Editors and Proprietors.

COL. J. H. BLOOD, Managing Editor.

All communications should be addressed

WOODHULL & CLAFLIN's WEEKLY,
Box 3,791, New York City.

The Principles of Social Freedom.

It has been said by a very wise person that there is a *trinity* in all things, the perfect *unity* of the trinity or a tri-unity being necessary to make a complete objective realization. Thus we have the theological Trinity: The Father, the Son and the Holy Ghost; or Cause, Effect and the Process of Evolution. Also the *political* Trinity: Freedom, Equality, Justice or *Individuality, Unity, Adjustment;* the first term of which is also resolvable into these parts, thus: Religious freedom, political freedom and social freedom, while Religion, Politics and Socialism are the Tri-unity of Humanity. There are also the beginning, the end and the intermediate space, time and motion, to all experiences of space, time and motion, and the diameter, circumference and area, or length, breadth and depth to all form.

Attention has been called to these scientific facts, for the purpose of showing that for any tri-unity to lack one of its terms is for it to be incomplete; and that in the order of natural evolution, if two terms exist, the third must also exist.

Religious freedom does, in a measure, exist in this country, but not yet perfectly; that is to say, a person is not entirely independent of public opinion regarding matters of conscience. Though since Political freedom has existed in theory, every person has the *right* to entertain any religious theory he or she may conceive to be true, and government can take no cognizance thereof—he is *only* amenable to *society-* despotism. The necessary corollary to Religious and Political freedom is Social freedom, which is the third term of the trinity; that is to say, if Religious and Political freedom exist, *perfected,* Social freedom is at that very moment guaranteed, since Social freedom is the fruit of that condition.

We find the principle of Individual freedom was quite dormant until it began to speak against the right of religious despots, to determine what views should be advocated regarding the relations of the creature to the Creator. Persons began to find ideas creeping into their souls at variance with the teachings of the clergy; which ideas became so *strongly* fixed that they were compelled to protest against Religious Despotism. Thus, in the sixteenth century, was begun the battle for Individual freedom. The claim that rulers had *no right* to control the consciences of the people was boldly made, and right nobly did the fight continue until the *absolute* right to individual opinion was wrung from the despots, and even the *common* people found themselves entitled to not only entertain but also to promulgate *any* belief or theory of which they could conceive.

With yielding the control over the *consciences* of individuals, the despots had no thought of giving up any right to their *persons*. But Religious freedom naturally led the people to question the right of this control, and in the eighteenth century a new protest found expression in the French Revolution, and it was baptized by a deluge of blood yielded by thousands of lives. But not until an enlightened people freed themselves from English tyranny was the right to self-government acknowledged in theory, and *not yet* even is it fully accorded in practice, as a legitimate result of that theory.

It may seem to be a *strange* proposition to make, that there is no such thing yet existent in the world as self-government, in its political aspects. But such is the fact. If self-government be the rule, every self must be its subject. If a person govern, not only *himself* but others, that is despotic government, and it matters not if that control be over one or over a thousand individuals, or over a nation; in *each* case it would be the *same* principle of power exerted outside of self and over others, and *this* is despotism, whether it is exercised by *one* person over his subjects, or by *twenty* persons over a nation, or by *one-half* the people of a nation over the other half thereof. There is no escaping the fact that the principle by which the *male* citizens of these United States assume to rule the *female* citizens is *not* that of self-government, but that of despotism; and so the fact is that poets have sung songs of freedom, and anthems of liberty have resounded for an empty shadow.

King George III. and his Parliament denied our forefathers the right to make their own laws ; they rebelled, and being successful, inaugurated this government. But men do not seem to comprehend that they are now pursuing toward *women* the *same* despotic course that King George pursued toward the American colonies.

But what is freedom? The press and our male governors are *very much* exercised about this question, since a certain set of resolutions were launched upon the public by Paulina Wright Davis at Apollo Hall, May 12, 1871. They are as follows:

Resolved, That the basis of order is freedom from bondage ; not, indeed, of such "order" as reigned in Warsaw, which grew out of the bondage ; but of such order as reigns in Heaven, which grows out of that developed manhood and womanhood in which each becomes "a law unto himself."

Resolved, That freedom is a principle, and that as such it may be trusted to ultimate in harmonious social results, as in America, it has resulted in harmonious and beneficent political results ; that it has not hitherto been adequately trusted in the social domain, and that the woman's movement means no less than the complete social as well as the political enfranchisement of mankind.

Resolved, That the evils, sufferings and disabilities of women, as well as of men, are social still more than they are political, and that a statement of woman's rights which ignores the right of self-ownership as the first of all rights is insufficient to meet the demand, and is ceasing to enlist the enthusiasm and even the common interest of the most intelligent portion of the community.

Resolved, That the principle of freedom is one principle, and not a collection of many different and unrelated principles ; that there is not at bottom one principle of freedom of conscience as in Protestantism, and another principle of freedom from slavery as in Abolitionism, another of freedom of locomotion as in our dispensing in America with the passport system of Europe, another of the freedom of the press as in Great Britain and America, and still another of social freedom at large ; but that freedom is one and indivisible ; and that slavery is so also ; that freedom and bondage or restriction is the alternative and the issue, alike, in every case ; and that if freedom is good in one case it is good in all ; that we in America have builded on freedom, politically, and that we cannot consistently recoil from that expansion of freedom which shall make it the basis of all our institutions ; and finally, that so far as we have trusted it, it has proved, in the main, safe and profitable.

Now, is there anything so terrible in the language of these resolutions as to threaten the foundations of society? They assert that every individual has a *better* right to herself or himself than any other person *can have*. No living soul, who does not desire to have control over, or ownership in, another person, can have any *valid* objection to *anything* expressed in these resolutions. Those who are not willing to give up control over others; who desire to *own* somebody beside themselves; who are constitutionally predisposed against self-government and the giving of the same freedom to others that they demand for themselves, will of course object to them, and such are the people with whom we shall have to contend in this new struggle for a greater liberty

Now, the individual *is* either self-owned and self-possessed or *is not* so self-possessed. If he be self-owned, he is so because he has an *inherent* right to self, which right cannot be delegated to any second person; a right—as the American Declaration of Independence has it—which is "inalienable." The individual must be responsible to self and God for his acts. If he be owned and possessed by some second person, then there is *no such thing* as individuality : and that for which the world has been striving these thousands of years is the merest myth.

But against this irrational, illogical, inconsequent and irreverent theory I boldly oppose the spirit of the age—that spirit which will *not* admit all civilization to be a failure, and all past experience to count for nothing; against that demagogism, I oppose the plain principle of freedom in its *fullest, purest, broadest, deepest* application and significance— the freedom which we see exemplified in the starry firmament, where whirl innumerable worlds, and never one of which is made to lose its individuality, but each performs its part in the grand economy of the universe, giving and receiving its natural repulsions and attractions; we also see it exemplified in every department of nature about us: in the sunbeam and the dewdrop; in the storm-cloud and the spring shower; in the driving snow and the congealing rain—all of which speak more eloquently than can human tongue of the heavenly *beauty, symmetry* and *purity* of the spirit of freedom which in them reigns untrammeled.

Our government is based upon the proposition that : All men and women are born free and equal and entitled to certain inalienable rights, among which are life, liberty and the *pursuit* of happiness. Now what we, who demand social freedom, ask, is simply that the government of this country shall be administered in accordance with the spirit of this proposition. *Nothing* more, *nothing* less. If that proposition mean *anything*, it means *just what* it says, without qualification, limitation or equivocation. It means that *every* person who comes into the world of outward existence is of *equal* right as an individual, and is free as an individual, and that he or she is entitled to pursue *happiness* in whatever direction he or she may choose. Now this is absolutely true of all men and all women. But just here the wise-acres stop and tell us that *everybody* must *not* pursue happiness in his or her own way; since to do so absolutely, would be to have no protection against the action of individuals. These good and well-meaning people only see *one-half* of what is involved in the proposition. They look at a single individual and for the time lose sight of all others. They do not take into their consideration that every other individual beside the one whom they contemplate is *equally* with him entitled to the *same* freedom; and that each is free within the area of his or her individual sphere; and *not* free within the sphere of any other individual whatever. They do not seem to recognize the fact that the moment one person gets out of *his* sphere into the sphere of *another*, that other must protect him or herself against such invasion of rights. They do not seem to be able to comprehend that the moment one person encroaches upon another person's rights he or she ceases to be a *free* man or woman and becomes a *despot.* To all such persons we assert: that it is *freedom* and *not* despotism which we advocate and demand; and we will as rigorously demand that individuals be restricted to *their* freedom as any person dare to demand; and as rigorously demand that people who are predisposed to be *tyrants* instead of free men or women shall, by the government, be so restrained as to make the exercise of their proclivities impossible.

If life, liberty and the pursuit of happiness are *inalienable* rights in the individual, and government is based upon that inalienability, then it *must follow* as a *legitimate* sequence that the *functions* of that government are to *guard* and *protect* the right to life, liberty and the pursuit of happiness, to the end that *every* person may have the most *perfect* exercise of them. And the most perfect exercise of such rights is *only* attained when every individual is not only fully *protected* in his rights, but also *strictly restrained* to the exercise of them within his *own* sphere, and *positively* prevented from proceeding beyond its limits, so as to encroach upon the sphere of another: unless that other first *agree* thereto.

From these generalizations certain specializations are deducible, by which all questions of rights must be determined :

1. Every living person has certain rights of which no law can rightfully deprive him.

2. Aggregates of persons form communities, who erect governments to secure regularity and order.

3. Order and harmony can alone be secured in a community where every individual of whom it is composed is fully protected in the exercise of all individual rights.

4. Any government which enacts laws to deprive individuals of the free exercise of their right to life, liberty and the pursuit of happiness is despotic, and such laws are not binding upon the people who protest against them, whether they be a majority or a minority.

5. When every individual is secure in the possession and exercise of all his rights, then every one is also secure from the interference of all other parties.

6. All inharmony and disorder arise from the attempts of individuals to interfere with the rights of other individuals, or from the protests of individuals against governments for depriving them of their inalienable rights.

These propositions are all self-evident, and must be accepted by every person who subscribes to our theory of government, based upon the sovereignty of the individual ; consequently any law in force which conflicts with any of them is not in accord with that theory and is therefore unconstitutional.

A fatal error into which most people fall, is, that rights are conceded to governments, while they are only possessed of the right to perform duties, as a further analysis will show :

In the absence of any arrangement by the members of a community to secure order, *each* individual is a law unto himself, so far as he is capable of maintaining it against all other individuals ; but at the mercy of all such who are bent on conquest. Such a condition is anarchy.

But if in individual freedom the *whole* number of individuals unite to secure *equality* and protection to themselves, they thereby surrender *no* individual rights to the community, but they simply *invest* the community with the power to perform certain specified *duties*, which are set forth in the law of their combination. Hence a government erected by the people is invested, *not* with the *rights* of the people, but with the *duty* of *protecting* and maintaining their rights *intact;* and any government is a *failure* or a *success* just so far as it fails or succeeds in this duty; and these are the legitimate functions of government.

I have before said that every person has the right to, and can, determine for himself what he will do, even to taking the life of another. But it is *equally* true that the attacked person has the right to defend his life against such assault. If the person succeed in taking the life, he thereby demonstrates that he is a *tyrant* who is at all times liable to invade the right to life, and that every individual of the community is put in jeopardy by the freedom of this person. Hence it is the *duty* of the government to so restrict the freedom of this person as to make it *impossible* for him to ever again practice such tyranny. Here the duty of the community ceases. It has *no* right to take the life of the individual. That is his own, *inalienably* vested in him, both by *God* and the *Constitution.*

A person may also appropriate the property of another if he so choose, and there is no way to prevent it; but once having thus invaded the rights of another, the whole community is in danger from the propensity of this person. It is therefore the duty of government to so restrain the liberty of the person as to prevent him from invading the spheres of other persons in a manner against which he himself demands, and is entitled to, protection.

The same rule applies to that class of persons who have a propensity to steal or to destroy the character of others. This class of encroachers upon others' rights, in some senses, are *more* reprehensible than any other, save only those who invade the rights of life; since for persons to be made to appear what they are not may, perhaps, be to place them in such relations with third persons as to destroy their means of pursuing happiness. Those who thus invade the pursuit of happiness by others, should be held to be the *worst* enemies of society; proportionably worse than the common burglar or thief, as what they destroy is more valuable than is that which the burglar or thief can appropriate. For robbery there may be *some* excuse, since what is stolen may be required to contribute to actual needs; but that which the assassin of character appropriates does *neither* good to himself nor to *any one else*, and makes the loser poor indeed. Such persons are the worst enemies of society.

I have been thus explicit in the analysis of the principles of freedom in their application to the common affairs of life, because I desired, before approaching the main subject, to have it *well settled* as to what may justly be considered the rights of individuals ; or in other words what individual sovereignty implies.

It would be considered a very unjust and arbitrary, as well as an unwise thing, if the government of the United States were to pass a law compelling persons to adhere during life to everything they should to-day accept as their religion, their politics and their vocations. It would *manifestly* be a departure from the true functions of government. The apology for what I claim to be an invasion of the rights of the individual is found in the law to enforce contracts. While the enforcement of contracts in which *pecuniary* considerations are involved is a matter distinct and different from that of the enforcement of contracts involving the happiness of individuals, *even in them* the government has *no* legitimate right to interfere. The logical deduction of the right of two people to *make* a contract without consulting the government, or any third party, is the right of *either or both* of the parties to *withdraw* without consulting any third party, either in reference to its enforcement or as to damages.

As has been stated, such an arrangement is the result of the exercise of the right of two or more individuals to unite their rights, perfectly independent of every outside party. There is neither right nor duty beyond the uniting—the contracting—individuals. So neither can there be an appeal to a third party to settle any difference which may arise between such parties. All such contracts have their legitimate basis and security in the honor and purposes of the contracting parties. It seems to me that, admitting our theory of government, no proposition can be plainer than is this, notwithstanding the practice is entirely different. But I am now discussing the abstract principles of the rights of freedom, which no practice that may be in vogue must be permitted to deter us from following to legitimate conclusions.

In all general contracts, people have the protection of government in contracting for an hour, a *day*, a *week*, a *year*, a *decade*, or a life, and *neither* the government nor *any other third* party or person, or *aggregates* of persons ever *think* of making a scale of respectability, graduated by the length of time for which the contracts are made and maintained. *Least of all* does the government require that any of these contracts shall be entered into for life. Why should the social relations of the sexes be made subject to a different theory? All enacted laws that are for the purpose of perpetuating conditions which are themselves the results of evolution are so many obstructions in the path of progress; since if an effect attained to-day is made the ultimate, progress stops. "Thus far shalt thou go, and no farther," is *not* the adage of a progressive age like the present. Besides, there can be no general law made to determine what individual cases demand, since a variety of conditions cannot be subject to one and the same rule of operation. Here we arrive at the most important of all facts relating to human needs and experiences: That while every human being has a distinct individuality, and is entitled to all the rights of a sovereign over it, it is not taken into the consideration that *no* two of these individualities are made up of the self-same powers and experiences, and therefore cannot be governed by the *same* law to the *same* purposes.

I would recall the attention of all objecting egotists, Pharisees and would-be regulators of society to the true functions of government—to protect the complete exercise of individual rights, and what they are no living soul except the individual has any business to determine or to meddle with, in *any* way whatever, unless his own rights are first infringed.

If a person believe that a certain theory is a truth, and consequently the right thing to advocate and practice, but from its being unpopular or against established public opinion does not have the moral courage to advocate or practice it, *that* person is a *moral coward* and a *traitor* to his own conscience, which God gave for a guide and guard.

What I believe to be. the truth I endeavor to practice, and, in advocating it, permit me to say I shall *speak* so *plainly* that *none* may complain that I did not make myself understood.

The world has come up to the present time through the outworking of religious, political, philosophical and scientific principles, and today we stand upon the *threshold* of *greater* discoveries in more *import-ant* things than have ever interested the intellect of man. We have arrived where the very *foundation* of all that *has* been must be ana-lyzed and understood—and this foundation is the relation of the sexes. These are the bases of society—the very last to secure attention, because the most comprehensive of subjects.

All other departments of inquiry which have their fountain in society have been formulated into *special* sciences, and made legitimate and popular subjects for investigation; but the science of *society itself* has been, and still is, held to be too sacred a thing for science to lay its rude hands upon. But of the relations of science to society we may say the same that has been said of the relations of science to religion: "That religion has always wanted to do good, and now science is going to tell it how to do it."

Over the sexual relations, marriages have endeavored to preserve sway and to hold the people in subjection to what has been considered a standard of moral purity. Whether this has been successful or not may be determined from the fact that there are *scores of thousands* of *women* who are denominated prostitutes, and who are supported by *hundreds of thousands* of *men* who should, for like reasons, also be de-nominated prostitutes, since what will change a woman into a prostitute must also necessarily change a man into the same.

This condition, called prostitution, seems to be the *great evil* at which religion and public morality hurl their *special* weapons of con-demnation, as the sum total of all diabolism; since for a woman to be a prostitute is to deny her not only all Christian, but also all humanita-rian rights.

But let us inquire into this matter, to see just what it is; not in the vulgar or popular, or even legal sense, but in a purely *scientific* and *truly moral* sense.

It must be remembered that we are seeking after truth for the *sake* of the truth, and in utter disregard of *everything* except the truth; that is to say, we are seeking for the truth, " let it be what it may and lead where it may. To illustrate, I would say the extremest thing possible. If blank materialism were true, it would be best for the world to know it.

If there be any who are not in harmony with this desire, then such have nothing to do with what I have to say, for it will be said regardless of antiquated forms or fossilized dogmas, but in the *simplest* and *least* offending language that I can choose.

If there is *anything* in the whole universe that should enlist the *earnest* attention of *everybody*, and their support and advocacy to secure it, it is that upon which the true welfare and happiness of everybody depends. Now to what more than to anything else do humanity owe their welfare and happiness? Most clearly to being born into earthly existence with a sound and perfect physical, mental and moral beginning of life, with no taint or disease attaching to them, either mentally, morally or physically. To *be so* born involves the harmony of conditions which will produce such results. *To have* such conditions involves the existence of such relations of the sexes as will in themselves produce them.

Now I will put the question direct. Are not these *eminently* proper subjects for inquiry and discussion, not in that manner of maudlin sentimentality in which it *has been* the habit, but in a *dignified, open, honest* and *fearless* way, in which subjects of so great importance should be inquired into and discussed ?

An *exhaustive* treatment of these subjects would involve the inquiry what should be the *chief* end to be gained by entering into sexual relations. This I must simply answer by saying, " Good children, who will not need to be regenerated," and pass to the consideration of the relations themselves.

All the relations between the sexes that are recognized as *legitimate* are denominated marriage. *But of what does marriage consist?* This very pertinent question requires settlement before any real progress can be made as to what Social Freedom and Prostitution mean. It is admitted by everybody that marriage is a union of the opposites in sex, but is it a principle of nature outside of all law, or is it a law outside of all nature ? Where is the point before reaching which it is not marriage, but having reached which it is marriage ? Is it where two meet and realize that the love elements of their nature are harmonious, and that they blend into and make *one* purpose of life ? or is it where a *soulless form* is pronounced over two who know *no* commingling of life's hopes ?

Or are *both* these processes required—first, the marriage union *without* the law, to be afterward solemnized *by* the law? If *both* terms are required, does the marriage continue after the *first* departs? or if the *restrictions* of the law are removed and the *love* continues, does *marriage* continue? or if the law unite two who *hate* each other, is that marriage? Thus are presented all the possible aspects of the case.

The *courts* hold if the law solemnly pronounce two married, *that they are* married, whether love is present or not. But is this really such a marriage as this enlightened age should demand? No! It is a stupidly arbitrary law, which can find no analogies in nature. Nature proclaims in *broadest terms*, and all her subjects re-echo the same *grand truth*, that sexual unions, which result in reproduction, are marriage. And sex exists wherever there is reproduction.

By analogy, the same law ascends into the sphere of and applies among men and women; for are not they a part and parcel of nature in which this law exists as a principle? This law of nature by which men and women are united by love is God's marriage law, the enactments of men to the contrary notwithstanding. And the precise results of this marriage will be determined by the character of those united; all the experiences evolved from the marriage being the legitimate sequences thereof.

Marriage must consist either of love or of law, since it *may* exist in form with either term absent; that is to say, people may be married by *law* and all love be lacking; and they may also be married by *love* and lack all sanction of law. True marriage must in reality consist entirely either of law or love, since there can be *no* compromise between the law of nature and *statute* law by which the former shall yield to the latter.

Law cannot change what nature has already determined. Neither will love obey if law command. Law cannot compel two to love. It has nothing to do either *with* love or with its absence. Love is superior to all law, and so also is hate, indifference, disgust and all other human sentiments which are evoked in the relations of the sexes. It legitimately and logically follows, if *love* have *anything* to do with marriage, that *law* has *nothing* to do with it. And on the contrary, if *law* have anything to do with marriage, that *love* has nothing to do with it. And there is no escaping the deduction.

If the test of the rights of the individual be applied to determine which of these propositions is the true one, what will be the result?

Two persons, a male and a female, meet, and are drawn together by a *mutual* attraction —a *natural* feeling unconsciously arising within their natures of which *neither* has any control—which is denominated love. This is a matter that concerns *these two*, and *no* other living soul has *any human* right to say aye, yes or no, since it is a matter in which none except the two have any right to be involved, and from which it is the duty of these two to exclude every other person, since no one can love for another or determine why another loves.

If true, mutual, natural attraction be sufficiently strong to be the *dominant* power, then it decides marriage ; and if it be so decided, no law which may be in force can *any more* prevent the union than a *human* law could prevent the transformation of water into vapor, or the confluence of two streams ; and for *precisely* the same reasons : that it is a *natural* law which is obeyed ; which law is as *high above human law* as perfection is high above imperfection. They marry and obey this higher law than man can make—a law as old as the universe and as immortal as the elements, and for which there is no substitute.

They are sexually united, to be which is to be married by nature, and to be thus married is to be united by God. This marriage is performed without special mental volition upon the part of either, although the intellect *may* approve what the affections determine; that is to say, they marry because they love, and they love because they can neither *prevent* nor *assist* it. Suppose after this marriage has continued an indefinite time, the *unity* between them departs, could they any more prevent it than they can prevent the love? It *came* without their bidding, may it not also *go* without their bidding? And if it go, does not the marriage cease, and should any third persons or parties, either as *individuals* or as *government*, attempt to compel the *continuance* of a unity wherein *none* of the elements of the union remain ?

At no point in the process designated has there been *any* other than an exercise of the right of the two individuals to pursue happiness in their *own* way, *which* way has neither *crossed* nor interfered with *any* one *else's* right to the *same* pursuit ; therefore, there is *no* call for a law to change, modify, protect or punish this exercise. It must be concluded, then, if individuals have the Constitutional right to pursue happiness in their *own* way, that all compelling laws of marriage and divorce are despotic, being *remnants* of the barbaric ages in which they were originated, and *utterly unfitted* for an age so *advanced* upon that, and so *enlightened* in the general principles of freedom and equality, as is this.

It must be remembered that it is the sphere of government to perform the *duties* which are required of it by the people, and that it has, in itself, no rights to exercise. These belong *exclusively* to the people whom it represents. It is *one* of the rights of a citizen to have a voice in determining what the duties of government shall be, and also provide how that right may be exercised; but government should not *prohibit* any right.

To love is a right *higher* than Constitutions or laws. It is a right which Constitutions and laws can *neither give* nor take, and with which they have nothing whatever to do, since in its *very* nature it is forever independent of both Constitutions and laws, and exists—comes and goes—in *spite* of them. Governments might just as well assume to determine how people shall exercise their right to *think* or to say that they shall not think at all, as to assume to determine that they shall not love, or how they may love, or that they shall love.

The proper sphere of government in regard to the relations of the sexes, is to enact such laws as in the present conditions of society are necessary to *protect each* individual in the *free* exercise of his or her *right* to love, and also to protect each individual from the forced interference of *every other* person, that would compel him or her to submit to *any* action which is against their *wish* and *will.* If the law do this it fulfills its duty. If the law do not afford this protection, *and worse still,* if it *sanction* this *interference* with the rights of an individual, then it is *infamous* law and worthy only of the *old-time* despotism; since individual tyranny forms *no* part of the guarantee of, or the right to, individual freedom.

It is therefore a strictly legitimate conclusion that where there is *no* love as a basis of marriage there should be *no* marriage, and if that which was the *basis* of a marriage is taken away that the *marriage* also ceases from that time, statute laws to the contrary notwithstanding.

Such is the character of the law that permeates nature from simplest organic forms—units of nucleated protoplasm to the most complex aggregation thereof—the human form. Having determined that marriage consists of a union resulting from love, without any regard whatever to the sanction of law, and consequently that the sexual relations resulting therefrom are strictly legitimate and natural, it is a very simple matter to determine what part of the sexual relations which are maintained are prostitutions of the relations.

It is certain by this Higher Law, that marriages of convenience, and, still more, marriages characterized by mutual or partial repugnance, are adulterous. And it does not matter whether the repugnance arises before or subsequently to the marriage ceremony. Compulsion, whether of the law or of a false public opinion, is detestable, as an element even, in the regulation of the most tender and important of all human relations.

I do not care where it is that sexual commerce results from the dominant power of *one sex* over *the other*, compelling him or her to submission against the *instincts of love*, and where hate or disgust is present, whether it be in the gilded palaces of Fifth avenue or in the lowest purlieus of Greene street, *there* is prostitution, and *all* the law that a *thousand* State Assemblies may pass cannot make it otherwise.

I know whereof I speak ; I have seen the most *damning* misery resulting from legalized prostitution. Misery such as the most degraded of those against whom society has shut her doors never know. Thousands of poor, weak, unresisting wives are yearly murdered, who stand in spirit-life looking down upon the sickly, half made-up children left behind, imploring humanity for the sake of honor and virtue to look into this matter, to look into it to the very bottom, and bring out into the fair daylight all the blackened, sickening deformities that have so long been hidden by the screen of public opinion and a sham morality.

It does not matter how much it may still be attempted to *gloss* these things over and to *label* them sound and pure ; you, each and every one of you, *know* that what I say is truth, and if you question your own souls you *dare* not reply : it is not so. If these things to which I refer, but of which I shudder to think, are not abuses of the sexual relations, what are?

You may or may not think there is help for them, but I say Heaven help us if *such* barbarism cannot be cured.

I would not be understood to say that there are no good conditions in the present marriage state. By no means do I say this; on the contrary, a very large proportion of present social relations are commendable—are as good as the present status of society makes possible. But what I *do* assert, and that most *positively*, is, that *all* which *is* good and commendable, now existing, would *continue* to exist if all marriage laws were repealed to-morrow. Do you not perceive that law has nothing to do in continuing the relations which are based upon continuous love? These are not results of the law to which, perhaps, their subjects yielded a willing or unwilling obedience. Such relations exist in *spite* of the law; would have existed *had there been* no law, and would continue to exist were the law *annulled.*

It is not of the *good* there is in the present condition of marriage that I complain, but of the *ill*, nearly the *whole* of which is the *direct* result of the law which continues the relations in which it exists. It seems to be the general argument that if the law of marriage were annulled it would follow that *everybody* must necessarily separate, and that all *present family* relations would be sundered, and complete anarchy result therefrom. Now, whoever makes that argument either does so thoughtlessly or else he is dishonest; since if he make it after having given any consideration thereto, he must know it to be false. And if he have given it no consideration then is he no proper judge. I give it as my opinion. founded upon an extensive knowledge of, and intimate acquaintance with, married people, if marriage laws were repealed that less than a *fourth* of those now married would immediately separate, and that *one-half* of these would return to their allegiance *voluntarily* within *one* year; only those who, under every consideration of virtue and good, should be separate, would permanently remain separated. And objectors as well as I know it would be so. I assert that it is *false* to assume that chaos would result from the abrogation of marriage laws, and on the contrary affirm that *from that very hour* the *chaos was* existing would *begin* to turn into order and Harmony. What then creates social disorder? Very clearly, the attempt to exercise powers over human rights which are not warrantable upon the hypothesis of the existence of human rights which are inalienable in, and sacred to, the individual.

It is true there is no *enacted* law compelling people to marry, and it is therefore *argued* that if they *do* marry they should always be compelled to abide thereby. But there is a law *higher* than any human enactments which does compel marriage—the law of nature— the law of God. There being this law in the constitution of humanity, which, operating freely, guarantees marriage, why should men enforce arbitrary rules and forms? These, though having no virtue in themselves, if not complied with by men and women, they in the meantime obeying the law of their nature, bring down upon them the condemnations of an interfering community. Should people, then, voluntarily entering legal marriage be held thereby "till death do them part?" Most *emphatically* NO, if the desire to do so do not remain. How can people who enter upon marriage in utter *ignorance* of that which is to render the union happy or miserable be able to say that they will always "love and live together." They may take these vows upon them in perfect good faith and repent of them in sackcloth and ashes within a twelvemonth.

I think it will be generally conceded that without love there should be no marriage. In the constitution of things *nothing* can be more certain. This basic fact is fatal to the theory of marriage for life: since if love is what *determines* marriage, so, also, should it determine its continuance. If it be primarily right of men and women to take on the marriage relation of their own free will and accord, *so*, too, does it remain their right to determine *how* long it shall continue and when it shall cease. But to be respectable (?) people must comply with the law, and thousands do comply therewith, while in their hearts they protest against it as an unwarrantable interference and proscription of their rights. Marriage laws that would be consistent with the theory of individual rights would be such as would *regulate* these relations, such as regulate *all other* associations of people. They should only be obliged to file marriage articles, containing whatever provisions may be agreed upon, as to their personal rights, rights of property, of children, or whatever else they may deem proper for them to agree upon. And whatever these articles might be, they should in all cases be equally entitled to public respect and protection. Should separation afterward come, nothing more should be required than the simple filing of counter articles

There are hundreds of lawyers who subsist by inventing schemes by which people may *obtain* divorces, and the people *desiring* divorces resort to *all sorts* of tricks and crimes to get them. And *all this* exists because there are laws which would *compel* the *oneness* of those to whom *unity* is beyond the realm of possibility. There are another class of persons who, while virtually divorced, endeavor to maintain a respectable position in society, by *agreeing* to *disagree*, each following his and her individual ways, behind the cloak of legal marriage. Thus there are *hundreds* of men and women who to *external* appearances are husband and wife, but in reality are husband or wife to quite different persons.

If the conditions of society were completely analyzed, it would be found that *all* persons whom the law holds married against their wishes find *some* way to *evade* the law and to live the life they desire. Of what use, then, is the law except to make *hypocrites* and *pretenders* of a sham respectability?

But, exclaims a very fastidious person, then you would have all women become prostitutes! By *no means* would I have *any* woman become a prostitute. But if by nature women *are* so, *all* the *virtue* they possess being of the *legal* kind, and not that which should exist with or without law, *then* I say they will not become prostitutes because the law is repealed, since at heart they are already so. If there is no virtue, no honesty, no purity, no trust among women except as created by the *law*, I say heaven help our morality, for nothing human can help it.

It seems to me that no grosser insult could be offered to woman than to insinuate that she is honest and virtuous only because the law compels her to be so; and little do men and women realize the obloquy thus cast upon society, and still less do women realize what they admit of their sex by such assertions. I honor and worship that purity which exists in the soul of every noble man or woman, while I pity the woman who is virtuous simply because a law compels her.

But, says another objector, though the repeal of marriage laws might operate well enough in all those cases where a *mutual* love or hate would determine *continuous* marriage or *immediate* divorce, how can a third class of cases be justified, in which but *one* of the parties desire the separation, while the other clings to the unity?

I assume, in the first place, when there is not mutual love there is no union to continue and nothing to justify, and it has already been determined that, as marriage should have love as a basis, if love depart marriage also departs. But laying this aside, see if there can any real good or happiness possibly result from an enforced continuance of marriage upon the part of one party thereto. Let all persons take this question home to their own souls, and there determine if they could find happiness in holding unwilling hearts in bondage. It is *against* the *nature of things* that *any* satisfaction can result from such a state of things except it be the satisfaction of knowing that you have succeeded in virtually imprisoning the person whom you *profess* to love, and that would be demoniacal.

Again. It must be remembered that the individual affairs of two persons are not the subject of interference by any third party, and if one of them choose to separate, there is no power outside of the two which can rightly interfere to prevent. Beside, who is to determine whether there will be more happiness sacrificed by a *continuation* or a *separation.* If a person is *fully* determined to separate, it is proof positive that another feeling *stronger* than all his or her sentiments of duty determine it. And here, again, *who* but the individual is to determine which course will secure the most good? Suppose that a separation is desired because one of the two loves and is loved elsewhere. In this case, if the union be maintained by force, at least *two* of three, and, probably, *all three* persons will be made unhappy thereby; whereas if separation come and the other union be consummated, there will be but one, unhappy. So even here, if the greatest good of the greatest number is to rule, separation is not only legitimate, *but* desirable. In all other things except marriage it is always held to be the right thing to do to *break* a *bad bargain* or *promise* just as soon as possible, and I hold that of *all things* in which this rule should apply, it should *first* apply to marriages.

Now, let me ask, would it not rather be the *Christian* way, in such cases, to say to the disaffected party: "Since you no longer love me, go your way and be happy, and make those to whom you go happy also." I know of no higher, holier love than that described, and of no more beautiful expression of it than was given in the columns of the *Woman's Journal*, of Boston, whose conductors have felt called upon to endeavor to convince the people that it has no affiliation with those who hold to no more radical doctrine of Free Love than they proclaim as follows:

"The love that I cannot command is not mine; let me not disturb myself about it, nor attempt to filch it from its rightful owner. A heart that I supposed mine has drifted and gone. Shall I go in pursuit? Shall I forcibly capture the truant and transfix it with the barb of my selfish affections, pin it to the wall of my chamber? God forbid! Rather let me leave my doors and windows open, intent only on living so nobly that the best cannot fail to be drawn to me by an irresistible attraction."

To me it is impossible to frame words into sentences *more holy, pure* and true than are these. I would ever carry them in my soul as my guide and guard, feeling that in *living* by them happiness would certainly be mine. To the loving wife who mourns a lost heart, let me recommend them as a panacea. To the loving husband whose soul is desolate, let me offer these as words of healing balm. They will live in history, to make their writer the *loved* and *revered* of unborn generations.

The tenth commandment of the Decalogue says: "Thou shalt not covet thy neighbor's wife." And Jesus, in the beautiful parable of the Samaritan who fell among thieves, asks: "Who is thy neighbor?" and answers his own question in a way to lift the conception wholly out of the category of mere local proximity into a sublime spiritual conception. In other words, he spiritualizes the word and sublimates the morality of the commandment. In the same spirit I ask now, Who is *a wife?* And I answer, not the woman who, ignorant of her own feelings, or with lying lips, has promised, in hollow ceremonial, and before the law, to love, but *she who really loves most,* and *most truly,* the man who commands her affections, and who in turn loves her, with or without the ceremony of marriage; and the man who holds the heart of such a woman in such a relation is "thy *neighbor*," and *that* woman is "*thy neighbor's wife*" meant in the commandment; and whosoever, though he should have been a hundred times married to her by the law, shall claim, or *covet* even, the possession of that woman as against her true lover and husband in the spirit, sins against the commandment.

We know positively that Jesus would have answered in that way. He has defined for us "the neighbor," not in the paltry and commonplace sense, but spiritually. He has said. "He that looketh on a woman to lust after her hath committed adultery with her already in his heart." So, therefore, he spiritualized the idea of adultery. In the kingdom of heaven, to be prayed for daily, to come on earth, there is to be no "marrying or giving in marriage;" that is to say, formally and legally; but spiritual marriage must always exist, and had Jesus been called on to define a wife, can anybody doubt that he would, in the same spirit, the spiritualizing tendency and character of all his doctrine, have spiritualized the marriage relation as absolutely as he did the breach of it? that he would, in other words, have said in meaning precisely what I now say? And when Christian ministers are no longer afraid or ashamed *to be Christians* they will embrace this doctrine. Free Love will be an integral part of the religion of the future.

It can now be asked: What is the legitimate sequence of Social Freedom? To which I unhesitatingly reply: Free Love, or freedom of the affections. "And are you a Free Lover?" is the almost incredulous query.

I repeat a frequent reply: "I am; and I can honestly, in the fullness of my soul, raise my voice to my Maker, and thank Him that *I am*, and that I have had the strength and the devotion to truth to stand before this traducing and vilifying community in a manner representative of that which shall come with healing on its wings for the bruised hearts and crushed affections of humanity."

And to those who denounce me for this I reply: "Yes, I am a Free Lover. I have an *inalienable, constitutional* and *natural* right to love whom I may, to love as *long* or as *short* a period as I can; to *change* that love *every day* if I please, and with *that* right neither *you* nor any *law* you can frame have *any* right to interfere. And I have the *further* right to demand a free and unrestricted exercise of that right, and it is *your duty* not only to *accord* it, but, as a community, to see that I am protected in it. I trust that I am fully understood, for I mean *just* that, and nothing less !

To speak thus plainly and pointedly is a *duty I owe* to myself. The press have stigmatized me to the world as an advocate, theoretically and practically, of the doctrine of Free Love, upon which they have placed their stamp of moral deformity: the vulgar and inconsequent definition which they hold makes the theory an abomination. And though this conclusion is a no more legitimate and reasonable one than that would be which should call the Golden Rule a general license to all sorts of debauch, since Free Love bears the *same* relations to the moral deformities of which it stands accused as does the Golden Rule to the Law of the Despot, yet it obtains among many intelligent people. But they claim, in the language of one of these exponents, that "Words belong to the people ; they are the common property of the mob. Now the common use, among the mob, of the term Free Love, is a synonym for promiscuity." Against this absurd proposition I oppose the assertion that words *do not* belong to the mob, but to that which they represent. Words are the exponents and interpretations of ideas. If I use a word which exactly interprets and represents what I would be understood to mean, shall I go to the *mob* and *ask* of *them* what interpretation *they* choose to place upon it ? If lexicographers, when they prepare their dictionaries, were to go to the mob for the rendition of words, what kind of language would we have ?

I claim that freedom means *to be free*, let the mob claim to the contrary as strenuously as they may. And I claim that love means an exhibition of the affections, let the mob claim what they may. And therefore, in compounding these words into Free Love, I claim that united they mean, and should be used to convey, their united definitions, the mob to the contrary notwithstanding. And when the term Free Love finds a place in dictionaries, it will prove my claim to have been correct, and that the mob have not received the attention of the lexicographers, since it will not be set down to signify sexual debauchery, and that only, or in any governing sense.

It is not only usual but also just, when people adopt a new theory, or promulgate a new doctrine, that they give it a name significant of its character. There are, however, exceptional cases to be found in all ages. The Jews coined the name of Christians, and, with withering contempt, hurled it upon the early followers of Christ. It was the most opprobrious epithet they could invent to express their detestation of those humble but honest and brave people. That name has now come to be considered as a synonym of all that is good, true and beautiful in the highest departments of our natures, and is revered in all civilized nations.

In precisely the same manner the Pharisees of to-day, who hold themselves to be representative of all there is that is good and pure, as did the Pharisees of old, have coined the word Free-Love, and flung it upon all who believe not alone in Religious and Political Freedom, but in that larger Freedom, which includes both these, Social Freedom.

For my part, I am extremely obliged to our thoughtful Pharisaical neighbors for the kindness shown us in the invention of so appropriate a name. If there is a more beautiful word in the English language than *love*, that word is *freedom*, and that *these two* words, which, with us, attach or belong to *everything* that is pure and good, should have been *joined* by our enemies, and *handed* over to us *already* coined, is certainly a high consideration, for which we should never cease to be thankful. And when we shall be accused of all sorts of wickedness and vileness by our enemies, who in this have been so just, may I not hope that, remembering how much they have done for us, we may be able to say, "Father, forgive them, for they know not what they do," and to forgive them ourselves with our whole hearts.

Of the love that says: "Bless *me*, darling;" of the love so called, which is nothing but selfishness, the appropriation of another soul as the means of one's own happiness merely, there is abundance in the world; and the still more animal, the mere desire for temporary gratification, with little worthy the name of love, also abounds. Even these are best left free, since as evils they will thus be best cured; but of that celestial love which says: "Bless *you*, darling," and which strives continually to confer blessings; of that genuine love whose office it is to bless others or another, there cannot be too much in the world, and when it shall be fully understood that this is the love which we mean and commend there will be no objection to the term Free Love, and none to the thing signified.

We not only *accept* our name, but we contend that *none* other could so well signify the *real* character of that which it designates—to be free and to love. But our enemies must be reminded that the fact of the existence and advocacy of such a doctrine cannot immediately elevate to high condition the great number who have been kept in degradation and misery by previous false systems. They must *not* *expect* at this early day of the new doctrine, that all debauchery has been cleansed out of men and women. In the haunts where it retreats, the benign influence of its magic presence has not yet penetrated. They must *not expect* that brutish men and debased women have as yet been touched by its wand of hope, and that they have already obeyed the bidding to come up higher. They must *not expect* that ignorance and fleshly lust have already been lifted to the region of intellect and moral purity. They must *not expect* that Free Love, before it is more than barely announced to the world, can perform what Christianity in eighteen hundred years has failed to do.

They must *not expect any* of these things have already been accomplished, but I will *tell* you what they *may* expect. They may expect *more* good to result from the perfect freedom which we advocate in *one century* than has resulted in a hundred centuries from all other causes, since the results will be in exact proportion to the extended application of the freedom. We have a legitimate right to predicate such results, since *all* freedom that has been practiced in *all* ages of the world has been beneficial *just* in proportion to the extent of human nature it covered.

Will any of you dare to stand up and assert that Religious Freedom ever produced a *single bad* result? or that Political Freedom *ever* injured a *single* soul who embraced and practiced it? If you can do so, then you may legitimately assert that Social Freedom *may* also produce *equally* bad results, but you cannot do otherwise, and be either conscientious or honest.

It is *too late* in the age for intelligent people to cry out *thief,* unless they have first been robbed, and it is equally late for them to succeed in crying down *anything* as of the devil to which a name attaches that angels love. It may be very proper and legitimate, and withal perfectly consistent, for philosophers of the *Tribune* school to bundle all the murderers, robbers and rascals together, and hand them over to our camp, labeled as Free Lovers. We will only object that they ought to hand the whole of humanity over, good, bad and indifferent, and not assort its worst representatives.

My friends, you see this thing we call Freedom is a large word, implying a deal more than people have ever yet been able to recognize. It reaches out its all-embracing arms, and while encircling our good friends and neighbors, does not neglect to also include their less worthy brothers and sisters, every one of whom is just as much entitled to the use of his freedom as is either one of us.

But objectors tell us that freedom is a dangerous thing to have, and that they must be its conservators, dealing it out to such people, and upon such matters, as they shall appoint. Having coined our name, they straightway proceed to define it, and to give force to their definition, set about citing illustrations to prove not only their definition to be a true one, but also that its application is just.

Among the cases cited as evidences of the evil tendencies of Free Love are those of Richardson and Crittenden. The celebrated McFarland-Richardson case was heralded world-wide as a case of this sort. So far as Richardson and Mrs. McFarland were concerned, I have every reason to believe it was a genuine one, in so far as the preventing obstacles framed by the "conservators" would permit. But when they assert that the murder of Richardson by McFarland was the *legitimate result* of Free Love, then I deny it *in toto*. McFarland murdered Richardson because he believed that the law had sold Abby Sage *soul* and *body* to him, and, consequently, that he *owned* her, and that *no* other person had *any* right to her favor, and that she had *no* right to bestow her love upon any other person, unless *that ownership* was first satisfied. The murder of Richardson, then, is not chargeable to his love or her love, but to the fact of the supposed ownership, which right of possession the law of marriage conferred on McFarland.

If anything further is needed to make the refutation of that charge clear, I will give it by illustration. Suppose that a pagan should be converted to Christianity through the efforts of some Christian minister, and that the remaining pagans should *kill* that minister for what he had done, would the crime be chargeable upon the Christian religion? Will any of you make that assertion? If not, neither can you charge that the death of Richardson should be charged to Free Love. But a more *recent* case is a still *clearer* proof of the correctness of my position. Mrs. Fair killed Crittenden. Why? Because she believed in the spirit of the marriage law; that she had a *better right* to him than had Mrs. Crittenden, to whom the law had granted him; and rather than to give him up to her, to whom he evidently desired to go, and where, following his right to freedom, he *did* go, she killed him. Could a more *perfect* case of the *spirit* of the marriage law be formulated? Most assuredly, no!

Now, from the standpoint of marriage, reverse this case to that of Free Love, and see what would have been the result had all those parties been believers in and practicers of that theory. When Mr. Crittenden evinced a desire to return to Mrs. Crittenden, Mrs. Fair, in practicing the doctrine of Free Love, would have said, "I have no right to you, other than you freely give; you loved me and exercised your right of freedom in so doing. You now desire to return to Mrs. Crittenden, which is equally your right, and which I must respect. Go, and in peace, and my blessing shall follow, and if it can return you to happiness, then will you be happy."

Would not *that* have been the *better*, the *Christian* course, and would not every soul in the broad land capable of a noble impulse, and having knowledge of all the relevant facts, have *honored* Mrs. Fair for it? Instead of a murder, with the probability of another to complement it, would not *all* parties have been *happy* in having done right? Would not Mrs. Crittenden have even *loved* Mrs. Fair for such an example of nobility, and could she not *safely* have received her even into her own heart and home, and have been a *sister* to her, instead of the means of her conviction of murder?

I tell you, my friends and my foes, that you have taken hold of the *wrong* end of this business. You are shouldering upon Free Love the results that flow from precisely its antithesis, which is the spirit, if not the letter, of your marriage theory, which is slavery, and not freedom.

I have a better right to speak, as one having authority in this matter, than most of you have, since it has been my province to study it in all its various lights and shades. When I practiced clairvoyance, *hundreds*, aye thousands, of desolate, heart-broken men, as well as women, came to me for advice. And they were from all walks of life, from the humblest daily laborer to the haughtiest dame of wealth. The tales of horror, of wrongs inflicted and endured, which were poured into my ears, first awakened me to a realization of the hollowness and the rottenness of society, and compelled me to consider whether laws which were prolific of so *much* crime and misery as I found to exist should be continued; and to ask the question whether it were not *better* to let the bond go free. In time I was fully convinced that marriage laws were productive of precisely the *reverse* of that for which they are supposed to have been framed, and I came to recommend the grant of entire freedom to those who were complained of as inconstant; and the frank asking for it by those who desired it. My *invariable* advice was: "Withdraw lovingly, but completely, all claim and all complaint as an injured and deserted husband or wife. You need not perhaps disguise the fact that you suffer keenly from it, but take on yourself all the fault that you have not been able to command a more continuous love; that you have not proved to be *all* that you once seemed to be. Show magnanimity, and in order to *show* it, try to *feel* it. Cultivate that kind of love which loves the happiness and well-being of your partner *most*, his or her person next, and yourself last. Be kind to, and sympathize with, the new attraction rather than waspish and indignant. Know for a certainty that love *cannot* be clutched or gained by being *fought* for; while it is not *impossible* that it may be won back by the nobility of one's own deportment. If it cannot be, then it is gone forever, and you must make the best of it and reconcile yourself to it, and do the next best thing—you may perhaps continue to *hold on* to a slave, but you have *lost* a lover."

Some may indeed think if I can keep the *semblance* of a husband or wife, even if it be not a lover, *better still* that it be so. Such is not my philosophy or my faith, and for such I have no advice to give. I address myself to such as have *souls*, and whose souls are in question ; if you belong to the other sort, take advice of a Tombs lawyer and not of me. I have seen a *few* instances of the most magnanimous action among the persons involved in a knot of love, and with the most angelic results. I believe that the love which goes forth to bless, and if it be to *surrender* in order to bless, is love in the *true* sense, and that it tends greatly to beget love, and that the love which is demanding, thinking only of self, is not love.

I have learned that the first *great* error most married people commit is in endeavoring to *hide* from each other the little irregularities into which all are liable to fall. *Nothing* is so conducive to continuous happiness as mutual confidence. In *whom*, if not in the husband or the wife, should one confide ? Should they not be each other's *best* friends, *never* failing in time of anxiety, trouble and temptation to give disinterested and unselfish counsel ? From such a perfect confidence as I would have men and women cultivate, it is *impossible* that bad or wrong should flow. On the contrary, it is the *only* condition in which love and happiness can go hand in hand. It is the *only* practice that can insure continuous respect, without which love withers and dies out. Can you not see that in mutual confidence and freedom the very *strongest* bonds of love are forged ? It is more blessed to grant favors than to demand them, and the blessing is large and prolific of happiness, or small and insignificant in results, just in proportion as the favor granted is large or small. Tried by this rule, the greater the *blessing* or happiness you can confer on your partners, in which your own selfish feelings are not consulted, the greater the satisfaction that will redound to yourself. Think of this mode of adjusting your difficulties, and see what a clear way opens before you. There are none who have once felt the influence of a high order of love, so *callous*, but that they *intuitively* recognize the true grandeur and nobility of such a line of conduct. It must always be remembered that you can never do *right* until you are first free to do *wrong ;* since the doing of a thing under *compulsion* is evidence *neither* of good nor bad intent; and if under compulsion, who shall decide what would be the substituted rule of action under full freedom?

In freedom *alone* is there safety and happiness, and when people learn this great fact, they will have just begun to know how to live. Instead then of being the destroying angel of the household, I would become the angel of purification to purge out all insincerity, all deception, all baseness and all vice, and to replace them by honor, confidence and truth.

I know very well that much of the *material* upon which the work must begin is very bad and far gone in decay. But I would have everybody perfectly free to do either right or wrong, according to the highest standard, and if there are those so unfortunate as not to know how to do that which can alone bring happiness, I would treat them as we treat those who are intellectually without culture—who are ignorant and illiterate. There are none so ignorant but they may be taught. So, too, are there none so unfortunate in their understanding of the true and high relation of the sexes as not to be amenable to the right kind of instruction. First of all, however, the would-be teachers of humanity must become truly Christian, meek and lowly in spirit, forgiving and kind in action, and ever ready to do as did Christ to the Magdalen. We are not so greatly different from what the accusing multitude were in that time. But Christians, forgetting the teaching of Christ, condemn and say, "Go on in your sin." Christians must learn to claim *nothing* for themselves that they are unwilling to accord others. They must remember that *all* people endeavor, so far as lies in their power, and so far as it is possible for them to judge, to exercise their human right, or determine what their action shall be, that will bring them most happiness; and instead of being *condemned* and *cast out* of society therefor, they should be *protected* therein, so long as others' rights are not infringed upon. We think they do not do the *best* thing; it is our duty to endeavor to *show* them the better and the higher, and to induce them to walk therein. But because a person chooses to perform an act that *we* think a *bad* one, we have no right to put the brand of excommunication upon him. It is our Christian and brotherly duty to persuade him instead that it is more to his good to do something better next time, at the same time, however, assuring him he only did what he had a right to do.

If our sisters who inhabit Greene street and other filthy localities *choose* to remain in debauch, and if our brothers *choose* to visit them there, they are only exercising the *same* right that we exercise in re-maining away, and we have no *more right* to abuse and condemn *them* for exercising their rights that way, than they have to abuse and con-demn us for exercising our rights our way. But we have a *duty*, and that is by our love, kindness and sympathy to endeavor to prevail upon them to desert those ways which we feel are so damaging to all that is high and pure and true in the relations of the sexes.

If these are the *stray sheep* from the fold of truth and purity, should we not go out and gather them in, rather than remain within the fold and hold the door shut, lest they should enter in and defile the fold? Nay, my friends, we have only an assumed right to thus sit in judgment over our unfortunate sisters, which is the same right of which men have made use to prevent women from participation in government.

The sin of all time has been the exercise of assumed powers. This is the essence of tyranny. Liberty is a great lesson to learn. It is a great step to vindicate our own freedom. It is more, far more, to learn to leave others free, and free to do just what we perhaps may deem wholly wrong. We must recognize that others have consciences and judgment and rights as well as we, and religiously abstain from the effort to make them better by the use of any means to which we have no right to resort, and to which we cannot resort without abridg-ing the great doctrine, the charter of all our liberties, the doctrine of Human Rights.

But the public press, either in real or affected ignorance of what they speak, denounce Free Love as the justification of, and apologist for, all manner and kind of sexual debauchery, and thus, instead of being the *teachers* of the people, as they *should* be, are the power which incul-cates falsehood and wrong. The teachings of Christ, whom so many now profess to imitate, were *direct* and simple upon this point. He was not too good to acknowledge all men as brothers and all women as sisters; it mattered not whether they were highly advanced in knowl-edge and morals, or if they were of low intellectual and moral culture.

It is seriously to be doubted if any of Christ's disciples, or men equally as good as were they, could gain fellowship in *any* of your Fifth avenue church palaces, since they were nothing more than the *humblest* of fishermen, of no social or mental standing. Neverthe‧less, they were *quite* good enough for *Christ* to associate with, and *fit* to be appointed by Him to be "fishers of men." The Church seems to have forgotten that good *does* sometimes come out of the Nazareths of the world, and that wisdom *may* fall from the mouths of "babes and sucklings." Quite *too much* of the old pharisaical spirit exists in society to-day to warrant its members' claims, that they are the repre‧sentatives and followers of Christ. For they are the I-am-holier-than‧thou kind of people, who affect to, and to a great extent do, prescribe the standards of public opinion, and who ostracise *everybody* who will not bow to their mandates.

Talk of Freedom, of equality, of justice! I tell you there is scarcely a *thought* put in practice that is *worthy* to be the offspring of those noble words. The *veriest systems of despotism* still reign in *all* matters pertaining to social life. Caste stands as boldly out in this country as it does in political life in the kingdoms of Europe.

It is true that we are obliged to accept the situation *just as it is.* If we accord freedom to all persons we must expect them to make their own best use thereof, and, as I have already said, must protect them in such use until they learn to put it to better uses. But in our predica‧tion we must be consistent, and now ask who among you would be *worse* men and women were *all* social laws repealed?

Would you *necessarily* dissolve your present relations, *desert* your dependent husbands—for there are even some of them—and wives and children simply because you have the *right* so to do? You are all trying to deceive yourselves about this matter. Let me ask of hus‧bands if they think there would be fifty thousand women of the town supported by them if their wives were ambitious to have an *equal* number of men of the town to support, and for the same pur‧poses? I tell you, nay! It is because men are held *innocent* of this support, and all the vengeance is visited upon the *victims*, that they have come to have an immunity in their practices.

Until women come to hold men to equal account as they do the women with whom they consort; or until they regard these women as just as respectable as the men who support them, society will remain in its present scale of moral excellence. A man who is well known to have been the constant visitor to these women is accepted into society, and if he be *rich* is eagerly *sought* both by mothers having marriageable daughters and by the daughters themselves. But the women with whom they have consorted are *too vile* to be even acknowledged as worthy of Christian burial, to say nothing of common Christian treatment. I have heard women reply when this difficulty was pressed upon them, " We cannot ostracise *men* as we are compelled to *women*, since we are *dependent* on them for *support.*" Ah! here's the rub. But do you not see that these *other* sisters are *also* dependent upon men for *their* support, and *mainly* so because you render it next to impossible for them to follow any *legitimate* means of livelihood ? And are only those who have been fortunate enough to secure *legal* support entitled to live ?

When I hear *that* argument advanced, my heart sinks within me at the degraded condition of my sisters. They submit to a degradation simply because they *see no alternative* except self-support, and they see no means for that. To put on the semblance of holiness they cry out against those who, for like reasons, submit to like degradation; the only difference between the two being in a licensed ceremony, and a slip of printed paper costing twenty-five cents and upward.

The good women of one of the interior cities of New York some two years since organized a movement to put down prostitution. They were, by stratagem, to find out who visited houses of prostitution, and then were to ostracise them. They pushed the matter until they found their own husbands, brothers and sons involved, and then suddenly desisted, and nothing has since been heard of the eradication of prostitution in that city. If the same experiment were to be tried in New York the result would be the same. The supporters of prostitution would be found to be those whom women cannot ostracise. The same disability excuses the presence of women in the very home, and I need not tell you that Mormonism is practiced in *other* places beside Utah. But what is the logic of these things ? Why, simply this ' A woman, be she wife or mistress, who consorts with a man who consorts with *other* women, is equally, with *them and him*, morally responsible, since the receiver is held to be as culpable as the thief.

The false and hollow relations of the sexes are thus resolved into the mere question of the *dependence* of women upon men for support, and women, whether married or single, are supported *by* men because they *are* women and their opposites in sex. I can see no moral difference between a woman who marries and lives with a man because he can provide for her wants, and the woman who is *not* married, but who is provided for at the same price. There is a *legal* difference, to be sure, upon one side of which is set the seal of respectability, but there is no virtue in law. In the *fact* of law, however, is the evidence of the lack of virtue, since if the law be *required* to enforce virtue, its real presence is wanting; and women need to comprehend this truth.

The sexual relation, must be rescued from this *insidious* form of slavery. Women must rise from their position as *ministers* to the passions of men to be their equals. Their entire system of education must be changed. They must be trained to be *like* men, permanent and independent individualities, and not their mere appendages or adjuncts, with them forming but one member of society. They must be the companions of men from *choice, never* from necessity.

It is a libel upon nature and God to say this world is not calculated to make women, equally with men, self-reliant and self-supporting individuals. In present customs, however, this is apparently impossible. There must come a change, and one of the direct steps to it will be found in the newly claimed political equality of women with men. This attained, one degree of subjugation will be removed. Next will come, following equality of right, equality of duty, which includes the duty of self-hood, or independence as an individual. Nature is male and female throughout, and each sex is equally dependent upon nature for sustenance. It is an infamous thing to say a condition of society which requires women to enter into and maintain sexual relations with men is their legitimate method of protecting life. Sexual relations should be the result of entirely different motives than for the purpose of physical support. The *spirit* of the present theory is, that they are entered upon and maintained as a *means* of physical gratification, regardless of the consequences which may result therefrom, and are administered by the dictum of the husband, which is often in direct opposition to the will and wish of the wife. She has *no* control over her own person, having been taught to "submit herself to her husband."

I protest against this form of slavery, I *protest* against the custom which compels women to give the control of their maternal functions over to anybody. It should be *theirs* to determine *when*, and under what circumstances, the greatest of all constructive processes—the formation of an immortal soul—should be begun. It is a *fearful* responsibility with which women are intrusted by nature, and the very *last* thing that they should be compelled to do is to *perform* the office of that responsibility against their will, under improper conditions or by disgusting means.

What can be more terrible than for a delicate, sensitively organized woman to be compelled to endure the presence of a beast in the shape of a man, who knows nothing beyond the blind passion with which he is filled, and to which is often added the delirium of intoxication? You do not need to be informed that there are many persons who, during the acquaintance preceding marriage, preserve a delicacy, tenderness and regard for womanly sensitiveness and modest refinement which are characteristic of true women, thus winning and drawing out their love-nature to the extreme, but who, when the decree has been pronounced which makes them indissolubly theirs, cast all these aside and reveal themselves in their *true* character, as without regard, human or divine, for aught save their own desires. I know I speak the truth, and you too know I speak the truth, when I say that thousands of the most noble, loving-natured women by whom the world was ever blessed, prepared for, and desirous of pouring their whole life into the bond of union, prophesied by marriage, have had all these generous and warm impulses thrust back upon them by the rude monster into which the previous gentleman developed. To these natures thus frosted and stultified in their fresh youth and vigor, life becomes a burden almost too terrible to be borne, and thousands of pallid cheeks, sunken eyes, distorted imaginations and diseased functions testify too directly and truly to leave a shade of doubt as to their real cause. Yet women, in the first instance, and men through them as their mothers, with an ignorant persistence worthy only of the most savage despotism, seem determined that it shall not be investigated; and so upon this voluntary ignorance and willful persistence society builds. It is *high* time, however, that they should be investigated, *high* time that your sisters and daughters should no longer be led to the *altar* like sheep to the shambles, in ignorance of the uncertainties they must inevitably encounter. For it is no slight thing to hazard a life's happiness upon a single act.

I deem it a false and perverse modesty that shuts off discussion, and consequently knowledge, upon *these* subjects. They are *vital*, and I never performed a duty which I felt *more* called upon to perform than I *now* do in denouncing as *barbarous* the ignorance which is allowed to prevail among young women about to enter those relations which, under present customs, as often bring a life-long *misery* as happiness.

Mistakes made in this most important duty of life can never be rectified ; a commentary upon the system which of itself is sufficient in the sight of common sense to forever condemn it. In marriage, how-ever, common sense is *dispensed* with, and a *usage* substituted there-for which barbarism has bequeathed us, and which becomes *more* barbarous as the spiritual natures of women gain the ascendancy over the mere material. The former slaves, before realizing that freedom was their God-appointed right, did not feel the *horrors* of their condi-tion. But when, here and there, some among them began to have an *interior* knowledge that they were held in obedience by an *unrighteous power*, they then began to *rebel* in their souls. So, too, is it with women. So long as they knew nothing beyond a blind and servile obedience and perfect self-abnegation to the will and wish of men, they did not rebel; but the time *has* arrived wherein, here and there, a soul is awakened by some terrible ordeal, or some divine inspiration, to the fact that women as much as men are *personalities, responsible* to them-selves for the use which they permit to be made of themselves, and they rebel demanding freedom, freedom to hold their own lives and bodies from the demoralizing influence of sexual relations that are not founded in and maintained by love. And this rebellion will continue, too, until love, unshackled, shall be free to go to bless the object that can call it forth, and until, when called forth, it shall be respected as holy, pure and true. Every day *farther* and wider does it spread, and *bolder* does it speak. None *too soon* will the yoke fall by which the unwilling are made to render a hypocritical obedience to the despotism of public opinion, which, distorted and blinded by a sham sentimentality, is a false standard of morals and virtue, and which is utterly destructive to true morality and to real virtue, which can only be fostered and cultivated by freedom of the affections.

Free Love, then, is the law by which men and women of all grades and kinds are attracted to or repelled from each other, and does not describe the results accomplished by either; these results depend upon the condition and development of the individual subjects. It is the *natural* operation of the *affectional* motives of the sexes, unbiased by *any* enacted law or *standard* of public opinion. It is the opportunity which gives the opposites in sex the conditions in which the law of chemical affinities raised into the domain of the affections can have unrestricted sway, as it has in *all* departments of nature *except* in enforced sexual relations among men and women.

It is an impossibility to compel incompatible elements of *matter* to unite. So also is it impossible to compel incompatible elements of *human nature* to unite. The sphere of chemical science is to bring together such elements as will produce harmonious compounds. The sphere of social science is to accomplish the same thing in humanity. Anything that stands in the way of this accomplishment in either department is an *obstruction* to the natural order of the universe. There would be just as much common sense for the chemist to write a law *commanding* that two incompatible elements should unite, or that two, once united, should so remain, even if a third, having a stronger affinity for one of them than they have for each other, should be introduced, as it is for chemists of society to attempt to do the same by individuals; for both are impossible. If in chemistry two properties are united by which the environment is not profited, it is the same law of affinity which operates as where a compound is made that is of the greatest service to society. This law holds in social chemistry; the results obtained from social compounds will be just such as their respective properties determine.

Thus I might go on almost infinitely to illustrate the difference which *must* be recognized between the operations of a law and the *law itself.* Now the whole difficulty in marriage law is that it endeavors to *compel* unity between elements in which it is impossible; consequently there is an attempt made to subvert not only the general order of the universe, but also the special intentions of nature, which are those of God. The results, then, flowing from operations of the law of Free Love will be *high, pure* and *lasting,* or *low, debauched and promiscuous, just in the degree* that those loving, are high or low in the scale of sexual progress; while each and all are strictly natural, and therefore legitimate in their respective spheres.

Promiscuity in sexuality is simply the *anarchical stage of development* wherein the passions rule supreme. When spirituality comes in and rescues the real man or woman from the domain of the purely material, promiscuity is simply impossible. As promiscuity is the analogue to anarchy, so is spirituality to scientific selection and adjustment. Therefore I am fully persuaded that the very highest sexual unions are those that are monogamic, and that these are perfect in proportion as they are lasting. Now if to this be added the fact that the highest kind of love is that which is utterly freed from and devoid of *selfishness,* and whose *highest* gratification comes from rendering its object the *greatest* amount of happiness, let that happiness depend upon whatever it may, then you have my ideal of the highest order of love and the most perfect degree of order to which humanity can attain. An affection that does not desire to bless its object, instead of appropriating it by a selfish possession to its own uses, is not worthy the name of love. Love is that which exists to *do* good, not merely to *get good,* which is constantly giving instead of desiring.

A Cæsar is admired by humanity, but a Christ is revered. Those persons who have lived and sacrificed themselves most for the good of humanity, without thought of recompense, are held in greatest respect. Christians believe that Christ died to save the world, giving His life as a ransom therefor. That was the greatest gift He could make to show His love for mankind.

The general test of love to-day is entirely different from that which Christ gave. That is now deemed the greatest love which has the strongest and most uncontrollable wish to be made happy, by the appropriation, and if need be the sacrifice, of all the preferences of its object. It says: "Be mine. Whatever may be your wish, yield it up to me." How different would the world be were this sort of selfishness supplanted by the Christ love, which says: Let this cup pass from me. Nevertheless, not my will but thine be done. Were the relations of the sexes thus regulated, misery, crime and vice would be banished, and the pale, wan face of female humanity replaced by one glowing with radiant delight and healthful bloom, and the heart of humanity beat with a heightened vigor and renewed strength, and its intellect cleared of all shadows, sorrows and blights. Contemplate this, and then denounce me for advocating Freedom if you can, and I will bear your curse with a better resignation.

Oh! my brothers and sisters, let me entreat you to have more faith in the self-regulating efficacy of freedom. Do you not see how beautifully it works among us in other respects? In America every-body is free to worship God according to the dictates of his own con-science, or even not to worship anything, notwithstanding you or I may think that very wicked or wrong. The respect for freedom we make paramount over our individual opinions, and the result is peace and harmony, when the people of other countries are still throtling and destroying each other to enforce their individual opinions on others. Free Love is only the appreciation of this beautiful principle of free-dom. One step further I entreat you to trust it still, and though you may see a thousand dangers, I see peace and happiness and steady improvement as the result.

To more specifically define Free Love I would say that I pre-fer to use the word *love* with *lust* as its antithesis, *love* representing the spritual and *lust* the animal; the perfect and harmonious inter-relations of the two being the perfected human. This use has its justification in other pairs of words; as good and evil; heat and cold; light and dark; up and down; north and south; which in *principle* are the same, but in *practice* we are obliged to judge of them as *relatively* different. The point from which judgment is made is that which we occupy, or are related to, individually, at any given time. Thus what would be up to one person might be down to another differently situated, along the line which up and down describe. So also is it of good and evil. What is good to one low down the ladder may not only be, but actually is, evil to one further ascended; nevertheless it is the same ladder up which both climb. It is the comprehension of this scientific fact that guarantees the *best* religion. And it is the *non-comprehension* of it that sets us as judges of our brothers and sisters, who are below us in the scale of development, to whom we should reach down the kind and loving hand of assistance, rather than force them to retreat farther away from us by unkindness, denunciation and hate.

In fine, and to resume: We have found that humanity is composed of men and women of all grades of development, from the most hideous human monster up to the highest perfected saint: that all of them, under our theory of government, are entitled to worship God after the dictates of their several consciences: that God is worshiped just as essentially in political and social thought and action as He is in religious thought and action; that no second person or persons have any right to interfere with the action of the individual unless he interfere with others' rights, and then only to protect such rights: that the thoughts and actions of all individuals, whether high and pure, or low and debauched, are equally entitled to the protection of the laws, and, through them, to that of all members of the community. Religious thought and action already receive the equal protection of the laws. Political thought and action are about to secure the equal protection of the laws. What social thought and action demand of the laws and their administrators is the same protection which Religion has, and Politics is about to have.

I know full well how strong is the appeal that can be made in behalf of marriage, an appeal based on the sanctions of usage and inherited respect, and on the sanctions of religion reinforced by the sanctions of law. I know how much can be said, and how forcibly it can be said, on the ground that women and especially that the children born of the union of the sexes, must be protected, and must, therefore, have the solemn contract of the husband and father to that effect. I know how long and how powerfully the ideality and sentiment of mankind have clustered, as it were in a halo, around this time-honored institution of marriage. And yet I solemnly believe that *all that* belongs to a dispensation of force and contract, and of a low and unworthy sense of mutual ownership, which is passing, and which is destined rapidly to pass, completely away ; not to leave us without love, nor without the happiness and beauty of the most tender relation of human souls; nor without security for woman, and ample protection for children; but to lift us to a higher level in the enjoyment of every blessing. I believe in *love with liberty; in protection without slavery; in the care and culture of offspring by new and better methods, and without the tragedy of self-immolation on the part of parents.* I believe in the family, *spiritually constituted,* expanded, amplified, and scientifically and artistically organized, as a unitary home. I believe in the most wonderful transformation of human society as about to come, as even now at the very door, through general progress, science and the influential intervention of the spirit world. I believe in more than all that the millennium has ever signified to the most religious mind ; and I believe that in order to prepare minds to contemplate and desire and enact the new and better life, it is necessary that the old and still prevalent superstitious veneration for the legal marriage tie be relaxed and weakened ; not to pander to immorality, but as introductory to a nobler manhood and a more glorified womanhood ; as, indeed, the veritable gateway to a paradise regained.

Do not criticise me, therefore, from a commonplace point of view. Question me, first, of the grounds of my faith. Conceive, if you can, the outlook for that humanity which comes trooping through the long, bright vista of futurity, as seen by the eyes of a devout spiritualist and a transcendental socialist. My whole nature is prophetic. I do not and cannot live merely in the present. Credit, first, the burden of my prophecy ; and from the new standing-ground so projected forth into the future, look back upon our times, and so judge of my doctrine ; and if, still, you cannot concede either the premises or the conclusion, you may, perhaps, think more kindly of me personally, as an amiable enthusiast, than if you deemed me deliberately wicked in seeking to disturb the foundations of our existing social order.

I prize dearly the good opinion of my fellow-beings. I would, *so gladly,* have you think well of me, and not ill. It is because I love you all, and love your well-being still more than I love you, that I tell you my vision of the future, and that I would willingly disturb your confidence, so long cherished, in the old dead or dying-out past. Believe me honest, my dear friends, and so forgive and think of me lovingly in turn, even if you are compelled still to regard me as deceived. I repeat, that I love you all; that I love every human creature, and their well being; and that I believe, with the profoundest conviction, that what I have urged in this discourse is conducive to that end.

Thus have I explained to you what Social Freedom or, as some choose to denominate it, Free Love, is, and what its advocates demand. Society says, to grant it is to precipitate itself into anarchy. I oppose to this arbitrary assumption the logic of general freedom, and aver that order and harmony will be secured where anarchy now reigns. The order of nature will soon determine whether society is or I am right. Let that be as it may, I repeat: The love that I cannot command is not mine; let me not disturb myself about it, nor attempt to filch it from its rightful owner. A heart that I supposed mine has drifted and gone. Shall I go in pursuit? Shall I forcibly capture the truant and transfix it with the barb of my selfish affection, and pin it to the wall of my chamber? Rather let me leave my doors and windows open, intent only on living so nobly that the best cannot fail to be drawn to me by an irresistible attraction."

CHAPTER 3

The Scare-crows of Sexual Slavery: An Oration

Introduced by Michael W. Perry

When Victoria Woodhull delivered this speech on August 17, 1873, she was still fuming over the political cartoon portraying her as "Mrs. Satan" that had been published in highly influential *Harper's Weekly* precisely eighteen months earlier to the very day and that's reproduced on the front cover of this book. In her opening words she can't seem to get that Satan accusation out of her head. She drew a line between her friends in the audience, whose good opinion she craved, and a broader public opinion, against which she asserted with a Christ-like authority, "Get thee behind me Satan." On the second page, she attacked religious opponents who "hold up a hell-fire and the Old Nick himself as scare-crows," while praising those who "not only seize hold of the straw hell and straw devil, but the inevitable straw God also, and hurl them in common ruin before the astonished world." She was clearly angry.

Having linked Satan and the devil to straw and scare-crows, Wood-hull went on to attack the "scare-crows" that were being used by "those who ape Popish power" (Catholicism) to frighten people away from free love. The first three scarecrows (pages 7-9) repeat arguments she dealt with in her speech on "The Principles of Social Freedom" (Chapter 2). The fourth, that children "wouldn't know their fathers," (10) was the objection her sister had raised at that speech. Finally, there's a fifth scare-crow, untitled and near the top of page 16, the fear that the freedom she promotes will lead to "license," with virtually everyone "indulging in the most outrageous extremes of all sorts of debauchery."

Woodhull answered with arguments similar to those she later used for government-controlled eugenics.[1] She claimed parents did not matter because most fathers and mothers are incompetent: "He is nothing but a poor excuse for a man; and she a worse one for a woman. He has spermatorrhea and she lencorrhea, and both are unfit to cohabit or reproduce themselves." She then attacked the condition of poor children, particularly in her own New York City. It was a risky step, since Woodhull was known for extravagant parties rather than for helping

---

1. See Victoria Woodhull, *Lady Eugenist: Feminist Eugenics in the Speeches and Writings of Victoria Woodhull* (Seattle: Inkling Books, 2005), 151f.

poor children, and many of her friends were financiers and industrialists who had grown rich exploiting the poor. But those were supporters whose concern ran no deeper than hers. In the decades to follow, a belief that many parents were unfit to have or rear children would create a zeal for eugenics and birth control, particularly among the well-to-do and well-educated, who had few or no children of their own.[2]

Woodhull went on to explain the future she envisioned, a society in which "there shall be no such thing as social slavery, now called the legal family in the world [marriage]; when the right of every woman to determine when and by whom she shall bear children shall be fully recognized and respected!" (11) Don't take that seriously. The essence of all eugenics is that some women do not have a right to become mothers. That eugenic agenda would be greatly advanced if, as Woodhull imagined further into her speech, women were paid by the State to breed children. (12) If the State is paying for children, the State will decide who can have them. And if there is "no such thing" as marriage, women will have no other stable, legally binding relationship in which to have children. They will stand alone against an all-powerful State.

Her first step in solving the 'father problem' was logical. Get rid of the economic need for a father, so that "in the new social order of society, women will be individually independent of men for support." (12) Marriage is equated with "sexual slavery," her term for mutual responsibility and a division of labor. "In place of this," Woodhull claimed, "it will be

---

2. Woodhull's supporters are described in Chapter 3 of *Lady Eugenist*. Those of birth control pioneer Margaret Sanger are in *The Pivot of Civilization in Historical Perspective*. A century later, Judith Blake found a similar pattern, noting, "Legalized abortion is supported most strongly by the non-Catholic, male, well-educated 'establishment.'" Judith Blake, "Abortion and Public Opinion: The 1960–1970 Decade," *Science*, 171 (February 12, 1971), 540–549. (The quote is on page 548.) Eugenics and birth control appear to have attracted more support among well-to-do women than legalized abortion, which may be why abortion proponents try so hard to frame it as a women's issue. The same was true of free love. When Woodhull made it a women's issue, she was being deceptive. Women had more to lose if marriage laws were weakened, while her wealthy male friends had the most to gain. Blake hints at a similar pattern for abortion legalization when she notes (p. 544) that for such men, "their sexual freedom has been curtailed, both within marriage and outside it, by restrictions on contraception and pregnancy termination, since as a class they are especially vulnerable to being held financially responsible for accidental pregnancies."

well understood that no man owes them anything, and that all their [sexual] intercourse will be governed by a maxim of equivalents in love." This scheme was no doubt popular with the rich, promiscuous men she associated with. "Equivalents in love" was just what they wanted. The brief romantic illusions created by soft words, red roses, and candle-lit dinners were cheaper than two decades of child support.

Of course Woodhull had not really solved the father problem. She neglected to mention that fathers play more roles than mere financial providers. But Woodhull was even-handed in her disdain for any parental role other than financial. At this point in her thinking, she intended to not only get rid of free love's father problem by eliminating fatherhood, she intended to rid society of other problems by eliminating motherhood. She described her solution this way:

> Next, when a woman becomes pregnant, it will be held immediately that she is laboring for society in the fact that she is to replenish its natural decrease. She will become the especial care of society and, while she is performing this sacred duty, be paid the highest wages received by any class, and be treated accordingly during the entire period of gestation and lactation, when the fruit of her labor [the baby] will of right belong to society and she return[s] to her common industrial pursuits. (12)

For Woodhull, women were breeding sows, laboring to "replenish" society's "natural decrease" through death. Their proper place—and she did have a place for them—was in "common industrial pursuits" and not at home baking cookies. Even early motherhood was factory work, a "labor" whose product "will of right belong to society." She also intended to make ordinary mothers and fathers feel guilty about their desire to be responsible, active parents, explaining how "thoughtless and inconsiderate" (12) it was for them to believe that their children belonged to them. By not relinquishing their son or daughter to an all-wise State, they were refusing what was best. Civilization and progress, Woodhull wrote, demands for the State "more and more of the conduct of the instruction of children," noting that for the State, "It is but one step beyond compulsory education to the complete charge of children." (13)

In this, as in many other areas, Woodhull was a pioneer. Today, some define progress in similar terms. For them, compulsory education in a badly run public school is 'better' for the mass of the people than allowing them to choose the content of their children's schooling through vouchers or similar plans. Of course, they exclude themselves from that sort of control, often placing their children in private schools.[3]

Woodhull, with two children of her own, knew children could not rear themselves. So she turned to the State for a child-rearing program she believed would be better than traditional parenting. For her, only one woman in ten was qualified for mothering. Most of the rest could labor in industry, improving the economic efficiency of society.

> The present theory makes a teacher and a nurse of every mother for life, and prevents her from acquiring or following any other occupation for which she may be fitted; while not more than one in ten have either the natural capacity or the necessary information to be either. Again, it compels all women to devote themselves almost wholly to domestic affairs, thus cutting them off from engaging in any other industrial calling—an incalculable loss as a question of economy, of industrial capacity, and limits the gross results of industry by an almost inconceivable amount. One-fifth of the women should readily perform the industry now performed by all women, leaving the other four-fifths to engage in other callings, and thus lessen the necessary hours for general toil all over the world. (14-15)

We can easily imagine Woodhull's friends in high finance purring almost as loudly at these words as her more radical socialist friends, who were as eager to see the State replace the family as they were to see the State replace private enterprise. In a traditional society, employers must pay fathers a "living wage" sufficient to support a wife and family or see the men migrate to better paying jobs. In Woodhull's world, employers would get two workers, a father and a former mother, for much same price they now paid for one. The messy business of child rearing, which did not fit well with their calculating mind set, would be done with what they thought was the greatest possible economic efficiency.

---

3. As I write this, the Court of Appeals for the Ninth Circuit has issued a ruling in *Fields v. Palmdale* (2005) in which a Judge Stephen Reinhardt closes with, "In summary, we hold that there is no free-standing fundamental right of parents 'to control the upbringing of their children by introducing them to matters of and relating to sex in accordance with their personal and religious values and beliefs' and that the asserted right is not encompassed by any other fundamental right." Compare that with the great zeal federal courts have displayed for creating a 'fundamental right' to abort that same child, and you'll see just how alive Woodhull's ideas are today.

The greater efficiency comes from the math behind Woodhull's child-rearing scheme. Imagine that the typical woman gives birth to three children, a number not quite sufficient to maintain the population in that era. That means the one-fifth who function as mother-substitutes must care for the offspring of five mothers or fifteen children. But the calculations do not end there. Those mother-substitutes are simply working at a job, so three eight-hour shifts will be needed to cover a 24-hour day (more if the "necessary hours for general toil" decrease as Woodhull claimed). We now have one mother-substitute caring for some 45 children each shift. If we assume for a moment with Woodhull that this substitute mothering works, it does signify an enormous increase in industrial productivity. One woman is doing the labor of fifteen.[4]

But at what cost will that productivity come? The core of Woodhull's argument is that most women are incompetent mothers—90 percent in fact. But she has already compromised herself by selecting 20 percent to be mother-substitutes, meaning that half are incompetent. Those figures grow worse if we assume that some good mothers will also be excellent surgeons or the like and would be best employed elsewhere. We now have mother-substitutes, perhaps three-fourths of them no more qualified than any other woman, caring for 45 children each. Obviously, these over-tasked mother-substitutes, even if they tried their best, could not produce the superior children Woodhull assumed would invariably result when she transferred child-rearing from parents to the State. Those children would be fortunate if any of these constantly changing mother-substitutes even learned their name.

So Woodhull's scheme, still alive today in a covert form that's more careful about what it says about parents, does not solve the many problems that free love has with a child's need for a mother and father. In the end, something more along the lines of Aldous Huxley's 1932 *Brave New World* would be necessary. In that world, you may remember, biological mothers and fathers do not exist. Everything is managed by experts called Controllers. Babies are grow in bottles to specifications set by the State, and everyone is conditioned to think only in ways that the State permits. Woodhull's strident call for individual sexual freedom,

---

4. With marvelously biting humor, G. K. Chesterton mocks this sort of industrialist in Chapter 11 of his 1922 *Eugenics and Other Evils* and deals equally harshly with the socialists in Chapter 15.

unchecked by common sense or experience, has led to a world of dreadful conformity that Huxley described in his opening words this way:

A squat grey building of only thirty-four stories. Over the main entrance the words CENTRAL LONDON HATCHERY AND CONDITIONING CENTRE, and, in a shield, the World State's motto, COMMUNITY, IDENTITY, STABILITY.

They could have easily added a fourth word to that motto, CONFORMITY. In Chapter 3, Huxley had someone explain what that conditioning meant with a sneer that might have delighted Woodhull.

Mothers and fathers, brothers and sisters. But there were also husbands, wives, lovers. There were also monogamy and romance.

"Though you probably don't know what those are," said Mustapha Mond.

They shook their heads.

Family, monogamy, romance. Everywhere exclusiveness, a narrow channelling of impulse and energy.

"But every one belongs to every one else," he concluded, citing the hypnopaedic proverb.

The students nodded, emphatically agreeing with a statement which upwards of sixty-two thousand repetitions in the dark had made them accept, not merely as true, but as axiomatic, self-evident, utterly indisputable.

Fortunately, none of us will have to listen to the Woodhull speech that follows repeated 62,000 times while we sleep, so we're less likely to regard it as "utterly indisputable." We can think, we can question the hidden assumptions, and we can work out the implications for ourselves, including linking them to their more veiled modern counterparts.

Time, a comfortable third marriage, and the respectability that followed, cooled Woodhull's anger at marriage and muted her call for free love. Perhaps she realized that getting rid of marriage altogether was too radical to win popular acceptance. Much better to weaken marriage to the point where it no longer posed a threat to the few who think it their right to manipulate birthrates and to control the rearing of other people's children. If so, then she remained to the end of her life thoroughly modern, fashionable and progressive.

THE

SCARE-CROWS

OF

SEXUAL SLAVERY,

AN ORATION

Delivered before fifteen thousand people, at Silver Lake, Mass.,
Camp Meeting, on Sunday, Aug. 17, 1873,

BY

VICTORIA C. WOODHULL.

————•◆•————

New York:
WOODHULL & CLAFLIN, PUBLISHERS.

1874.

The Scare-Crows of Sexual Slavery.

My Brothers and Sisters.—I am going to tell you some plain truths to-night. I know I shall not please all your ears. I value the good opinion of you all, but I value the truth more, and if to gain the former I must withhold one iota of the latter I shall fail in securing it. Your good opinion I crave, for I feel that you are my friends—friends to the great human race, and he or she who is this, though they hate me with a deadly hatred, is my friend; but public opinion I stamp in the mud. It is a stench in the nostrils of truth, for which, if any care, he must say, "Get thee behind me, Satan?" I will not so much as vary a single hair's breadth from what I conceive to be my duty, though public opinion should turn the faces of every man and woman against me. I will speak the truth, I will be heard; but you may kill me afterward if you will. I have but one sentiment in my soul, and that is to do what in me lies to lift up the down-trodden and enslaved of earth, and to inaugurate equality and happiness in the world. I have no kindred, less than the human race, who demand or can have service of me. My life is dedicated to this work, and I come to you to speak such words as will make your souls sink in horror and your curses to rest upon yourselves, that you have so long quietly permitted these things to go on unrebuked. I would, if it were possible, wring from you the declaration that you would know no rest again until these wrongs be righted. It must come to this. The world is to be made free and beautiful, and happy because so, and methinks I can see in the not distant future, a time when misery and heartaches and poverty and all unhappiness shall be banished the earth, and the entire human family, both in earth and spirit life, fully and harmoniously united, singing the glad songs of the redeemed. But before this can be, other and terrible things must be. So much suffering as the soul-sick sons and daughters of earth now suffer, cannot be transformed to bright and happy conditions, without the atoning blood of, I had almost said, millions of martyr souls.

Let the sacrifice be what it may, however, it must be paid, and heaven help all of them, who love their brothers and sisters all over the world, to endure what must be endured. Having thus briefly alluded to what I shall say to you, I will proceed to speak upon

THE SCARE CROWS OF SEXUAL SLAVERY.

If a stranger visit the farming districts of the New England States in the month of June, he will observe in many newly-planted corn-fields the most hideous-looking objects, fashioned after the human form. They occupy the prominent positions about the field, as if standing sentry over the young corn. And so they are; but a view from the highway only, may not show of what these improvised sentinels are composed, other than that they wear the external garb of a dilapidated individual, who, not having much money to spend, spends the most of this for that which is said to make some feel rich and others to forget that they are poor. If, however, the boy with the inevitable "little brown jug" happen to come along at this juncture, from him it may be learned that the sentinels are men of straw merely, stationed there as a warning to the crows from yonder wood, against venturing into the field to pull up the newly planted corn, the sprouts from which are beginning to make the fields look green.

But now observe upon what the efficiency of these men of straw depends. There they stand motionless, with not so much as the power to raise a hand for harm or good; but the crows, having just sense enough to see in them the resemblance to their great enemy—man—carefully avoid coming within their domain; and thus through ignorance is the young corn saved.

But scare-crows are found in other than corn fields, and for other purposes than to save young corn. They are found in the religious field. Those who have commanded here, in order to save their realm, hold up a hell-fire and the Old Nick himself as scare-crows, to prevent the ignorant and the foolish from invading their possessions, or rather from exploring beyond them. Since all people, however, are not crow people, they do not always succeed. Some have been bold enough to move right onward, and not only seize hold of the straw hell and straw devil, but the inevitable straw God also, and hurl them all in common ruin before the astonished world. Some cry out "Sacrilege!" while others quietly remark, "Well, it was only a blind after all. Strange that we could have been fooled so long by these fellows who ape Popish power."

In the field of politics there are the same class who invent scare-crows with which to fool the people—their serfs—one of the most terrible of which, at the present, is that of a woman voting, and the idea of justice for industry. These are, indeed, terrific sights, enough to blanch the face of such as, all their lives, have lived under the rod of male domination and the money god, and the belief that man is the natural lord of creation altogether, when every sensible woman knows she belies herself by this admission, since she also should know that she may be the absolute monarch over man, able to compel him upon his knees to supplicate for, instead of presuming to grant favor. Oh! woman, hast thou not yet learned thy subtle yet potent power, that thou doth still grovel in mean servility at the feet of thy serf, if thou wouldst have him so!

This naturally introduces the social field, whose scare-crows it is our special province at this time to consider. I know them all to be "men of straw" merely, that the lightest puff, the slightest breath of truth will topple over and expose to the world, if it will but look on them as they fall.

Before we begin this destruction, to pull them in pieces to learn of what they are made, let us find if we can, and may, what is the occasion that has called the pretended lords of this field to erect them, and also forestall the criticism that would otherwise be clutched from our simile of the corn field, the distinction to be made between which and the field of sexual freedom being this: While those who plant the corn and erect the straw men to preserve its growth in the former instance, in the latter, reverse the order. The enemy invade the fields where we have sown the seeds of social reform, which are just beginning to make its withered and whitened surface look green again, and on our ground erect these scare-crows to prevent the crows, the ignorant among people, from coming to partake of the feast of gladness that is here spread We trust the enemy will take this distinction home with him and carefully bestow it in his memory, so that he may not make himself doubly foolish after a while by the introduction of the criticism for which this is intended as an antidote.

But what is all this about? Well, it is a part of the contest between despotism and freedom. Absolutism on the one hand, representing the former, and individual sovereignty on the other hand representing the latter. This contest is not so much a strife between opposites, however, as it is an effort on the part of despots to prevent their subjects from becoming freemen. In the evolution of civilization the people walk in the path of progress, taking a departure from despotism toward freedom, which is at the other extreme of civilization.

The original question to be considered, then, is as to which of these extremes of civilization is the proper one, at which an enlightened people should halt, and upon which they should frame their institutions? Having departed from absolutism—the one-man power—there is no possible halting-place that can be permanent, until democracy—the sovereignty of every individual—is reached. If this be true as a general proposition, it is equally so as a proposition of every department of civilization. If individual sovereignty is a principle of right in matters of conscience—the religious field—it must be so also in politics. It is impossible that a law found to be natural to one phase of life, should be unnatural to every or any other phase of life. If individual sovereignty is the law of religion and of politics, it is also the law of the social relations: and there is no method of argumentation by which an escape from this conclusion is possible.

Individual sovereignty means freedom for the individual; then if there is any meaning in the logic of events for the last hundred years, freedom for the individual, socially, is an inherent right of which neither he or she can be deprived rightfully, by any power whatever, whether it be of Church or State, or of both combined.

Nobody will doubt this, but many will now ask, what is freedom? And if the definition given do not quite meet with their ideas of propriety and respectability, they will reject it as heresy, the right of sovereignty to the contrary notwithstanding.

Freedom, in general terms, means simply this: that each and every individual has the right in his or her own proper person to make such use of any or all his powers and capacities as he or she may elect to do. Anything less than this is not freedom—it is restriction, and restriction exercised by any person or aggregate of persons over another person is despotism, but the rule of social order must be either freedom or despotism: it cannot be a mixture of both.

Immediately this proposition is made, scare-crow No. **1 is** presented to affright the inquirer, and this declares: If everybody be given the right to do just as they wish, anybody would not be safe a moment anywhere. Every saint will be robbed, outraged or murdered by some sinner, and anarchy itself would hold high carnival, while civilization would sink in the blackness of the dark ages.

Now let us not imitate the crow, and fight shy of this scare, but walk straight in its face, and pull off its mask, and tear down its pretense. In the first place the short-sighted wiseacres who pre nd to be frightened out of their wits at the thought of freedom, do not see if the right of each individual to freedom be guaranteed, that this alone is perfect protection for everybody; since if everybody have this right secure, he is safe from every interference from another person. If, then, the freedom of any person whatever, is interfered with, it is the fault of the organization of society which causes it to fail to secure every individual of whom it is composed in the possession of his freedom, and not the fault in any sense or shape of the right of freedom itself.

First, there are the individuals composing the community, each of whom is entitled to freedom; and second, there is the organization of the community, which is, or should be, made specifically to secure the rights of every individual, inalienable to him. Again we repeat: If it do not do this, it is the fault of the community, and not a denial of the right or justice of freedom. So here even at the first great bugbear that stands threatening every one who seeks to know about this important word, freedom, it is found that the very thing which it is sought to retain by the denial of freedom—protection for individual rights—can only be secured beyond all peradventure by the guarantee of freedom to everybody.

No sooner, however, than No. 1 is demolished, than instantly No. 2 is put forward. "Well," says the objector, 'suppose it be admitted that it is right for every individual to have his or her freedom, it is not expedient that it should be exercised entirely free from restraint." Expediency is the great scare-crow No. 2; but it is even more fatally faulty than No. 1, though a deal more dangerous. Many a person will admit that it may be right for him or her to possess freedom and to exercise it, but they don't exactly know whether it will be quite safe to trust the neighbors with it. It is exceedingly doubtful as to the use they will make of it, and it might not be just the thing, "you know." There's no telling; they might do some very naughty things; and if they all should do just what they might do, why the whole community would be demoralized, and the foundations of society undermined, and that, oh! that would be terrible."

But let this class of objectors be pinned down so it may be known where they are and where they belong, in order that it may be known what it is at which we are aiming our shots. Now, sir, do you mean to affirm or deny that I have the right to think and act as I choose; to eat, drink and sleep as I may; to go here, there, or wherever I desire; to love this, that or the other as I can—do you say that I have the right to determine these things for myself, or do you say that somebody else has the right to determine them for me? Do you, in fact, affirm or deny individual freedom or communal and individual despotism? That's the question, and please don't dodge it, but meet it squarely. Is it freedom or the opposite? Never as yet have we been able to compel anybody who denies freedom to affirm despotism? Can we do it now, sir, with you?

"Well, now, I really don't imagine that it would be right for me to say that I or anybody else has the right to have anything whatever to do with these things of which you speak; but you know society must protect itself, must regulate things in some way, or else what would become of us all?"

Now, this is just the point, Mr. Objector. It is simply none of your business what other people do; nor any of the business of society what any of its members do, unless they interfere with somebody else without his or her consent; and you and all like you might as well learn this fact here and now as later; since your system of meddling interference with that which is none of your business will not be longer tolerated. If freedom be a right possessed by all individuals, it cannot matter what use may be made of it. It must be adopted as the basic principle, and be assured that the results will take care of themselves. Having adopted freedom as opposed to despotism, all its logical deductions are also adopted. It is impossible that anything founded on truth should result in error. If the foundation be right the structure built upon it will not fall from any basic defects.

' But," replies the objector, "I cannot understand about this business. If there be no law to compel people to live together, everything will be in confusion, the family will be broken up; and this is the safeguard of society, morality and everything else that is good and pure. Everything will go to the bad directly if it be not maintained by all the safeguards that can be thrown around it. No! no! It will never do to break up the family."

SCARE-CROW NO. 3.

And thus scare-crow No. 3 is elevated to be in turn demolished. To begin, we deny in toto everything you have said. The very safeguards that you have thrown around the family to make it pure and holy have made instead, a community of little hot hells, in which the two principals torment each other until one or the other gives up the contest, and by which the seeds of devilism are sown in all the children who may unfortunately for themselves and society, result. These safeguards to virtue and morality have made almost every wife a prostitute and every husband a sexual monster, and compels them both, against their better natures, to continually go from bad to worse.

Compel people to live together, would you? Of all the monstrous propositions, this is the most monstrous. As a theory, it is absurd enough; but as a practice it is simply revolting infernalism. Even the condition of prostitutes, of which there is so much pretended commiseration, is to be preferred to this! They have the right to refuse to cohabit when they choose; but the poor wife is denied even this. She must submit or take a thrashing, perhaps! Why, sir, your safeguards are the allies o hell, and are responsible for more misery, more sickness and more crime than all other causes combined; and humanity as a whole, perhaps as yet unconsciously, cries to its God for deliverance. Be assured this cry will be heard and answered. For the sake of consistency, sir, you would do well to take in your family scare-crow before you and your like become utterly obnoxious.

"But," says the objector, "suppose I do, what will become of the children? If the family be left free to be broken up, they will be at the mercy of the world, not knowing who are their fathers even—a terrible dilemma, surely!"

SCARE-CROW No. 4.

This is scare-crow No. 4. Wouldn't know their fathers! Ah! that would be bad; a fearful state of things, wouldn't it? Now, do you really mean that as an objection; do you wish it to be understood that you are in earnest? You must be attempting to play a joke upon somebody! Why, sir, there isn't a person in the world who knows absolutely who his father is! There may be many who perhaps *think* they know; but thought has deceived many a one in other things, and undoubtedly has in this one as well. It is not safe, only to think, in a matter where it is assumed that positive certainty is necessary. To my certain knowledge there are some persons who think they know their fathers who are wonderfully at fault in thus thinking. Indeed is marriage a safeguard in some ways that ye wot not of; but they are all right, "you know,"—that is, so long as they are not found out.

But in the highest respect to the order of things, what does it matter whether the child, or any one, knows who is its father? Answer this, with reason, who can! Is he or is society any better for this knowledge? Are they any better men and women because of it? Is it not rather to be feared that the questions of real value, both to children and society, are overlooked in the false importance given such as this—such as are of no value whatever to anybody, except of harm? The great error of civilization is in this question of children, and the simple yet sublime doctrines of the Nazarene can never be inaugurated in the world until it is corrected.

What will become of the children, indeed? A pretty question to ask is this, when next to nothing is now done to prevent them from going to the bad! Look at the children! What are they but a scraggy, scrawny, half made up lot! and again at the way through which they grow to maturity! Which of them at that time is really worth calling a man or a woman? He is nothing but a poor excuse for a man; and she a worse one for a woman. He has spermatorrhea, and she leucorrhea, and both are unfit to cohabit or to reproduce themselves; and yet you talk about the children. Why, sir, you must be beside yourself.

Why do you not, in place of asking what will become of the children, ask what is becoming of them now? Go ask the fifty thousand houseless, half starved, wholly untaught children of of New York city, who live from the swill-barrels of the rich Christians, what is becoming of them, and they will tell you they don't know!   But it will be plain to be seen that they are going to the bad, surely.   I cannot understand how it is that the critics of social freedom should be so terribly concerned about the children who are to be, when they have no concern whatever for those who are.   Solicitude for children, when there are five millions of people in the United States, one-eighth of the total population, over ten years of age, who can neither read nor write ! Why, it is simply absurd!   There is no such thing.   This pretended solicitude is something pumped up in the imaginations of these idealists as a scare-crow to prevent inquirers after freedom from finding the direct road.

If there were any such thing as solicitude for children, it would show itself in having the conditions in which they are begotten of the most favorable character.   The mother, during pregnancy, would be treated as if she were preforming the divinest mission of nature, where now she is too often treated more like a slave.   Thousands of poor weak women are to-day performing the task of maternity, who are also compelled to labor, to the utmost extent of their strength, for their daily bread, and perhaps also to feed a drunken tyrant to whom the law has made her slave, both sexually and industrially.   Care for children! Again I repeat it, they who pretend this must be fools or insane, or else think that you are both, that they may play upon you such a pretense as this.

Passing all these points, however, we have a right to reply to the query, What will become of the children when there shall be no such thing as social slavery, now-called the legal family in the world ;   when the right of every woman to determine when and by whom she shall bear children shall be fully recognized and respected ?   We have a right to answer this I say, since if there is to be no change for the better over the present, then the scare-crow of expediency might have real force, and operate as a hindrance to the establishment of the reign of social democracy.   But if it cannot be determined exactly, what will become of the children !   That fact should not be held an obstacle to freedom, if it be proved that freedom itself is right.   The conditions under which children are begotten and raised, are certainly about as bad as they can well be.   Since they are the results of the social system, their condition should not be taken as an indication of what children ought to be under an entirely opposite order ; nor as an objection to the establishment of such an order.   Inaugurate the new order, and the method of rearing children will be determined by the new conditions of that order.

In the first place, however, in the new social order of society, women will be individually independent of men for support. From the beginning it will be known that they are not to be educated as sexual slaves for man, merely. In place of this, it will be well understood that no man owes them anything, and that all their intercourse will be governed by a maxim of equivalents in love. It may be necessary to inform men, but it is not to inform women, that in such conditions there will be no undesired pregnancy ; whereas, now, four-fifths of the children who are born are unwelcomed.

Next, when a woman becomes pregnant, it will be held immediately that she is laboring for society in the fact that she is to replenish its natural decrease. She will become the especial care of society and, while she is performing this sacred duty, be paid the highest wages received by any class, and be treated accordingly during the entire period of gestation and lactation, when the fruit of her labor will of right belong to society and she return to her common industrial pursuits.

I know that this by the thoughtless will be considered almost a heartless proposition, since there is no love like a mother's love for her child. It will, however, be found, if patience permit the full consideration, that what is proposed will give the very greatest scope for the exhibition of the mother's love. It must not be lost sight of that the first thing to be gained by a revolution in our present social system is better men and women ; and if a mother's love can in any way interfere with this result, then it should not be permitted to do so.

But before going further, a grave error that exists almost universally should be corrected. It is thoughtlessly and inconsistently held that the children belong to their parents, and because it is so held, it is the most dangerous question with which the reformer has to deal ; but at the same time, of the very first importance. To say that children do not belong to their parents, is to attack a supposed right that has existed from time immemorial, and to call down upon the head of the attacking party the reprobation even of radicals. I am after the truth, however, and let it be what it may and lead where it may I shall pursue it mercilessly, well knowing that when found it will doubly repay all the expense incurred, if that be even complete ostracism.

I would not, however, ruthlessly wound or shock any tender

mother s heart. I would rather show her that her love, if it be really worthy of that divine name, will incline her to desire for her child that which will make it the best man or woman. Now I ask every mother present if this is not what the love of every mother ought to desire ; and also further, if, in desiring this, any selfish love that she bears merely for her own sake, regardless of the good of her child, ought not to be ignored in the higher consideration of its best interests and through it of society ? Every true mother will answer, yes! without hesitation ; only those who would sacrifice their children to their own selfish love will even hesitate.

A single question will, however, show the absurdity of the theory of ownership. If parents own their children, how does it come that they ever lose their title, as they do at adult age ; or again, and still more forcibly, if the title of children is in their parents, how is it that society, by its laws, claims them when, before adult age, they commit some crime ; or still again, to whom is this ownership transferred when the parents die ; and again, how is it that society compels the education of children? If they belong to their parents, what right has society to meddle? Answer these and then say if you can that children do not belong to society.

It is well known that, as civilization progresses and education becomes more a question of public interest, society demands more and more the conduct of the instruction of children. Public schools are now imperative, where, but a hundred years ago, there was no such system. Compulsory education is already adopted in some States, and is being seriously considered as a national measure. It is but one step beyond compulsory education to the complete charge of children. If society have the right to say how and how much a child shall be educated mentally, it certainly has the right, also, to say what the other processes of education shall be.

Indeed, it is more than a right. It is a duty that society owes to those whom it is to make amenable to its regulations, that they shall have the best possible preparation to assume the duties and the responsibilities of citizenship and equals ; and still more a duty, that all children should become citizens, having received equal opportunities of preparation, so that no man, by his superior culture, shall be able to enslave others of less acquirements, either industrially, intellectually, or in any other manner whatever. Who shall dare say, if all children should be reared according to the theory of M. Godin's Industrial Palace, at Guise, France, that they would not be better men and women than those are who have been reared under our present theory of parental ownership?

What will become of the children? Again, what does become of them? One-half of all children cut off by death before the age of five years—a commentary on the pretended anxiety for children that seems more like a horrible tragedy. Think of it, mothers! fathers! reformers! One-half of all children dying before they reach five years of age—victims of our present social system, of the prevailing ignorance of the science of sexuality and the needs of the young, and of the theory of parental ownership! The world cannot afford to suffer this terrible loss. When a ship founders at sea, with the loss of a few hundred lives, the whole country is aroused over the horror; but it sleeps quietly over the fact that double that number of children —babes, almost—fall victims daily to the fell destroyers, ignorance and superstition and false social customs.

Infancy and childhood should be the healthiest period of life, but it is ten times more fatal than any other that can be selected with which to institute a comparison. There is but one verdict that can be rendered over these untimely deaths, and this is: Died at the age of from three days to four years, of maternal ignorance; or, to put it more plainly: Murdered by the ignorance of mothers. This is strikingly apparent when it is remembered that, as soon as this period is passed and children begin to take care of themselves somewhat, the death rate decreases almost immediately. Think of this again, ye mothers, before you shall utterly condemn a system that will save all these precious buds of promise to you and to the world.

The present theory makes a teacher and a nurse of every mother for life, and prevents her from acquiring or following any other occupation for which she may be fitted; while not more than one in ten have either the natural capacity or the necessary information to be either. Again, it compels all women to devote themselves almost wholly to domestic affairs, thus cutting them off from engaging in any other industrial calling—an incalculable loss as a question of economy, of industrial capacity, and limits the gross results of industry by an almost inconceivable amount. One-fifth of the women should readily perform the industry now performed by all women, leaving the other four-fifths to engage in other callings, and thus lessen the necessary hours for general toil all over the world.

Many proposed reforms may seem to be questionable—may appear to be right upon principle, but utterly wrong as a matter of policy ; but in this one of children, both right and expediency join hands in demanding it, and they should reiterate the demand in thunder tones until the sleepy world is awakened to its dire necessity. And should social freedom be much longer hampered by restricting laws, then there will be the greater need of this change, in the matter of children. Society cannot permit one-half its children to be murdered by the ignorance of their mothers. Childhood, I repeat, of all periods of life, should be the freest from disease ; but as it is now managed it is by far the most fatally afflicted. Again I say, a comment upon present methods that transposes them into horrible tragedies, and stamps the crime of murder upon every household.

But what may seem more strange than anything that has yet been said, is that these are really the doctrines of Jesus put to practice. He taught, or is said to have taught, the universal love that the adoption of such a system as is referred to would necessarily develop. The logical result of this is that a parent will love the children of others as well as he does his own, which, in other words, is loving his neighbor as he does himself and those of his own household. Relationship in the future will be based upon kindredness of spirit rather than upon ties of blood ; while family clanship, like all similar cliqueisms, the remnants of barbarism, will be forever banished the earth.

Do professing Christians believe the teachings of the "Master?" There is no mistaking the authority of these. They are clearly the doctrines of the Lord Jesus, whom they profess to wish to become their temporal as well as spiritual ruler. Dispute this who can, assumptions to the contrary notwithstanding; and escape the condemnation who may, pharisaical godliness to the defense, nevertheless.

It is claimed, therefore, that in whatever case, whether it be in matters of religion, politics, or social life ; or again in matters of duty, the individual only has the sovereign power ; and that any interference with this, by any force of any kind, that does not operate upon him through change to his convictions, is despotism, and altogether opposed to freedom. Everybody, then, is free to act his own life ; and no individual, nor any number of individuals, has any right, except that of might, to compel him differently. Some may feel it their duty to endeavor to change the methods of others lives, but at last the individual must be left free to do as he will—and this is the practice of the theory of individual freedom ; the only point from which general progress can ever possibly begin and continue indefinitely.

We have not yet disposed of all the scare-crows, and the next one that is erected to frighten the people, of freedom. is license—a most terrible spectre indeed, one from which the multitude falls back in dismay, almost convinced that it is impossible to discover freedom where this monster stands guard over the way. This monster assumes, if all restriction to liberty be removed, that license is thereby granted to everybody to do all sorts of bad things, and that a great many people will immediately proceed to do all these bad things.

First of all, every woman, except those of our household, will incontinently go to the bad, indulging in the most outrageous extremes of all sorts of debauchery; while the men, everybody excepting "ourselves" of course, will also incontinently proceed to commit rape upon every woman who is so unfortunate as to fall in their way. Age of either extreme will fail to command respect when men are free, and terror and horror will reign triumphant. So much for the assumptions.

But hold, dear sir. Are you not making yourself just a little rediculous? Did you not say that all the women would immediately rush into the arms of every man they should meet, let it be in the street, in the car or wherever else; that even negroes would not escape the mad debauch of white women ? Now observe. If this be so, upon whom are these outrages, by men, to be committed? Do you not see if every woman is of her own accord to rush to debauchery, that it will be entirely unnecessary for men to resort to any sort of force whatever, or even to resort to persuasion. A splendid commentary on wo-woman, indeed. Are you not proud of it, my sisters ?

But, for the argument's sake, suppose that every woman and every man, except those of your household, on acquiring freedom, should rush into utter promiscuousness in their sexual relations, is it not their perfect right to do so ? And who should have the right to say nay ? Indeed, your assumption is that almost everybody will be included in this debauch. Shall not the large majority rule ? Shall the transcendent purity of the "ten" interfere to prevent the "million" from prosecuting their right to the pursuit of happiness, sexually ? Are there any constitutional, any natural rights upon which phariseeism shall not lay its meddling hands? I have yet to learn either that you have the right, or the might even, if you had the right, to do anything except to mind your own business. What is it to you whether I live upon fish or flesh?

Such conceptions of freedom as you present only succeed in showing one thing effectually; and this is, that, when freedom is gained, its subjects had better look to the holders of there opinions for the first outrage. Why should the matter of sex, wherever involved, be held to different rules from every other passion? For murder, theft and arson, there are laws to punish the crimes, leaving the people perfectly free to commit them if they will. Anybody who should propose restricting laws, after the theory of marriage laws, to apply to anything else than sex, would be voted a fool, and that, too, by the most persistent sticklers for the same theory as applied to sex. All the laws that can be made regarding sex, and be in harmony with the general theory, maintained in everything else, are such as would punish sexual intercourse obtained by force—in other words, rape; and this is the end of the whole question. There is no more need of a marriage law on account of the children, than there is of a law regarding theft, fashioned after the same theory, on their account; and any wayfaring man, though a fool, should be able to see this.

License in love where consent is made a necessary qualification, by the guarantee of freedom to women to refuse, if they will, is simply an absurdity. They who raise it as an objection, and place it in the field of freedom to scare away the foolish crows, know it to be a bare-faced fraud. If we were not too charitably inclined to permit such a thing, we might conceive that the people who cry out against freedom, as synonymous with license, do so in order to secure to themselves all, that under other conditions, might accrue to others—a scare-crow set up to keep everybody else away while the "knowing ones" pull up the corn.

If the system of restrictory marriage laws, as now practiced, is such a preventative to sexual crime as it is pretended that it is, how is it that there is so much sexual virtue before these laws come into force? How is it that unmarried men and women are so free from what opponents call sexual crime? Opponents will not pretend that this is otherwise than I present it. They will not say there is none of their sort of virtue before marriage. But what does this prove? Why, the most complete condemnation and utter refutation of the whole system, that can be invented. It proves unavoidably and conclusively that marriage, instead of freedom, is the hot-bed of license. Marriage, licenses sexuality, while nothing else does; and the horrors that are practiced under this license, are simply demoniacal; almost too horrible to be even thought of without shuddering, how much more so to relate! There is nothing else but marriage that licenses a man to debauch a woman against her will. There is no sexual license except in marriage.

But those who would save this institution by force, having attempted to defend it, and thereby having invited us to the contest, we must not hesitate to drag from their hiding-places the terrific skeletons that marriage has left in almost every household; and it must be expected that it will be done mercilessly. This infamous system that murders one-half the children in babyhood and three-fourths of the mothers, and robs almost all the rest of all happiness in this life, shall not, if it can be helped, be tolerated any longer. I have declared relentless warfare against it, and by the help of heaven, it shall be waged until the last vestige of this remnant of savagery shall be wiped from the otherwise fair face of present civilization.

Going a little backward to the early days of abolitionism, it is found that the same system of warfare that is now proposed was waged by the heroes of that freedom. They not only attacked slavery upon the question of abstract right, but they also attacked it in the concrete, in its practices. Individual instances of cruelty, as well as the general tendency of the system, were pointed out and depicted with all the terrible effect of truth. Individual offenders were compelled into the light and held up to public detestation, and were made a by-word to the fullest possible extent. The public sensibilities were shocked by actual and vivid pictures of whatever atrocities the slaveholding system developed. Many people cried shame! and denounced it as scandalous, stopping their ears and eyes lest themselves should be shocked at the knowledge that such things could be in a civilized country, and pretended to share all their sympathy with the real offender for being driven to the light, just as if it were not a thousand times worse that such things should be enacted at all. But the brave warriors rushed on in spite of their criticisms and their sensibilities until at last the institution fell, and nobody now dare say they were wrong or that aught but good has resulted ; but they repeat the error nevertheless.

Now through just such experiences have the holders of sexual slaves got to be compelled. All the horrors of this slavery will have to be dragged to the light, and whenever individual offenders can be caught they must be exposed. All this may be seemingly hard ; nevertheless it is the only method by which the atrocities to which the system has given birth, can be unearthed, and its own foundation shattered. Many are the tales of horror and brutal violence that have been related of negro slavery, where the lash of the driver was depicted until their hearers almost felt its stings in their own flesh, and almost the red streams flowing down their own backs, and these appealed to the souls of men and women until they were ready to do whatever was needed to destroy a monster that could cause such suffering to a single human being. But I am fully convinced that all the suffering of all the negro slaves combined, is as nothing in comparison to that which women, as a whole, suffer. There were several millions of negro slaves. There are twenty millions of women slaves. The negroes were dependent upon their masters for all the comforts of life they enjoyed; but it was to the interest of their masters to give them all of these that health demanded. Women are as much dependent upon men for their sustenance as were the negroes upon their masters, lacking the interest that they had in the negroes as personal property.

It is an unpleasant thing to say that women, in many senses, are as much slaves as were the negroes, but if it be true, ought it not to be said ? I say, a thousand times, yes! And when the slavery to which they are subjected is compared to that which the negro endured, the demand for its consideration increases again, still a thousand times more.

Perhaps it may be denied that women are slaves, sexually, sold and delivered to man. But I tell you, as a class, that they are, and the conclusion cannot be escaped. Let me convince all doubters of this. Stand before me, all ye married women, and tell me how many of you would remain mistresses of your husbands' homes if you should refuse to cohabit sexually with them ? Answer ye this, and then tell me that ye are free, if ye can ! I tell ye that you are the sexual slaves of your husbands, bound by as terrible bonds to serve them sexually as ever a negro was bound to serve his owner, physically; and if you don't quite believe it, go home and endeavor to assert your freedom, and see to what it will lead! You may not be made to feel the inevitable lash that followed rebellion on the part of the negro, but even this is not certain; yet lashes of some sort will surely be dealt. Refuse to yield to the sexual demands of your legal master, and ten to one he will turn you into the street, or in lieu of this, perhaps, give you personal violence, even to compelling you to submit by force. Tell me that wives are not slaves! As well might you have done the same of the negroes, who, as the women do not, did not realize their condition!

I offer it as a well-grounded conclusion that I have come to, after years of inquiry and observation, that nine of every ten wives, at some time during their marriage, are compelled, according to the injunction of St. Paul, to submit themselves to their husbands, when every sentiment of their souls revolts at the act; and I feel an answering response coming up to me from many sick souls among you, that shrink in horror from the contemplation of the terrible scenes to which they have been compelled.

Remember, I do not say this is universally true; I do not say that all wives, at all times, are thus situated. Neither were all negro slaves at all times subjected to the lash or to other brutal treatment. The large majority of negroes were well treated and comparatively happy; but they were slaves, nevertheless. The cases of extreme cruelty were really rarer than is generally believed, but they were enough to condemn the system and to cause its terrible washing out by the blood of hundreds of thousands of the brightest souls of the country. So, also, are the cases of extreme cruelty on the part of husbands not exceedingly common, but they are sufficiently so to condemn the whole system, and to demand, if need be, that it, too, be washed out by the blood, if necessary, of millions of human beings.

For my part I would rather be the labor slave of a master, with his whip cracking continually about my ears, my whole life, than the forced sexual slave of any man a single hour; and I know that every woman who has freedom born in her soul will shout in deepest and earnest response to this—Amen! I know what it is to be both these. I have traveled the icy pavements of New York in mid-winter, seeking employment, with nothing on my feet except an old pair of india-rubber shoes, and a common calico dress only to cover my body, while the man who called me wife and who made me his sexual slave, spent his money upon other women. I am not speaking whereof I know not. My case may be thought an extreme one, but I know of thousands even worse. Then tell me I shall not have the right to denounce this damned system! Tell me I shall be sent to Sing Sing if I dare expose these things! Open your Sing Sings a thousand times, but none of their terrors shall stop a single word. I will tell the world, so long as I have a tongue and the strength to move it, of all the infernal misery hidden behind this horrible thing called marriage, though the Young Men's Christian Association sentence me to prison a year for every word. I have seen horrors beside which stone walls and iron bars are heaven, and I will not hold my peace so long as a system, that can produce such damnation and by which, as its author, heaven is blasphemed, exists.

Would to Heaven I could thunder these facts forth until women should be moved by a comprehension of the low degradation to which they have fallen, to open rebellion; until they should rise *en masse* and declare themselves free, resisting all sexual subjection, and utterly refusing to yield their bodies up to man, until they shall grant them perfect freedom. It was not the slaves themselves who obtained their own freedom. It was their noble white brothers of the North, who, seeing their condition, and realizing that though they were black, still that they were brothers, sacrificed themselves for the time to emancipate them. So it will not be the most suffering slaves of this horrible slavery who will accomplish its abolition; but it must be those who know and appreciate the terrible condition, who must, for the time, sacrifice ourselves, that their sisters may come to themselves and to own themselves.

Go preach this doctrine, then, ye who have the strength and the moral courage: No more sexual intercourse for men who do not fully consent that all women shall be free, and who do not besides this, also join the standard of the rebellion. It matters not if you be wife or not, raise your voice for your suffering sex, let the consequences to yourself be what they may. They say I have come to break up the family; I say amen to that with all my heart. I hope I may break up every family in the world that exists by virtue of sexual slavery, and I feel that the smiles of angels, the smiles of those who have gone on before, who suffered here what I have suffered and what thousands are suffering, will give me strength to brave all opposition, and to stand even upon the scaffold, if need be, that my sisters all over the world may be emancipated, may rise from slavery to the full dignity of womanhood.

I ought not to need to resort to details. Every family has its skeleton, which, if exposed to public view, would scarcely seem worse than its neighbor. Every wife's life is a tragedy, and would every woman stand up and tell her experiences in legal sexual slavery, the stones beneath your feet would cry out in anguish at the recital. But it must come to this at last. Women, if they would be saviors, must be willing to tell the world what they have suffered, and through this the revolution will come. Marriage-slavery has slaughtered more women than ever there were men slaughtered on the gory fields of battle. I have heard their stories until my soul is sick with the horror. I could rehearse cases to you till morning that would harrow up your very souls and awaken you to a sense of the infamies that are perpetrated in the name and under cover of this monstrous thing. I will tell you but one.

A sister of a friend died recently. She married, four years ago, a clergyman of the City of New York. At that time she was in the bloom of vigorous health. She was a beautiful woman both in form and feature, and seemed to have been fashioned in nature's choicest mold to be capable of enjoying all the blessings of physical life. She possessed a deep love-nature and had amativeness largely developed, which under any reasonable condition, would have reciprocated the requirements of any person. But this clergyman was scarcely human in his sexual demands. His brutal approaches, when first married, made sexual reciprocity impossible for her. He knew but one thing—selfish gratification, and was oblivious to everything else. She was his tool, used by him with no recognized rights of her own. The complete stultification of her sexual nature at the very outset began to undermine her health, and by the time she had her third child she was a doomed woman. When on her death-bed, her sister, who was heart-broken over the death she knew was shortly to come, went one day to her bedside and implored her to tell her what had caused this terrible destruction. She replied: "My sister, for the good of the world I will tell you, although I had thought to go down to my grave carrying the secret with me; but the story of my life may save many a poor wife from my horrible fate. I have sacrificed my life to what I have erroneously believed to be my religious duty."

But I cannot, even with my courage, relate this as it came to me from this sister. It amounted to this however: This husband was merely a sexual animal, and never knew satiety. As many as from six to ten times a day did he compel this poor woman to submit to him. The special periods of every woman's life did not exempt her from this slavery, nor when she was performing the functions of gestation did he relent, but pursued her even up to the birth of the children, and within two days thereafter, absolutely forced her to his desires. She concluded her story by saying: "Sister, this is the cause of my death. Say to the world I was murdered by the legal right which marriage gave to this man whom I have called husband, and whom I believed it my duty to obey or else be doomed to hell. I would not live longer if I could. I have prayed that death might come every day since I was married, and now it is coming to set me free," and almost immediately she expired.

Brothers and sisters: This may be an extreme case, but it stands for marriage throughout, and in modified form will express the history of many a woman cut off in the same way. I know of hundreds of similar cases. Then do you wonder that I cannot hold my peace? Do you not rather wonder that I can contain myself as well as I have? And yet almost everybody condemns me for justifying the promiscuous intercourse with many women, of a man who, like this clergyman, has inordinate sexual demands. Would it not have been better, for this human fiend, to have expended his sexuality among the members of his church, provided they had desired it, and would have been made happier by it; and if they had not, then with so-called prostitutes for hire, rather than to have murdered his poor wife as he did? Think of this before you again condemn the attempt on the part of anybody to establish an equilibrium in sexual things. Excessive amativeness in men must find its balance in women, and an equilibrium be thereby established, before there can be harmony.

This poor woman was a Christian, and believed her only way to escape hell was to obey old Paul's injunction. I say, damn such Christianity as that; and I know it is damned and doomed to be sunk into the lowest pit of hell, from whence it shall never again be resurrected to torture the life out of foolish Christian women.

But I turn sick at heart from the contemplation of the horror; by which marriage is enveloped, to consider some of the conditions to which the future will lead. In the first place, women will have to proclaim a declaration of independence, to be maintained, if necessary, with their lives, forever establishing their freedom sexually, as against any and all requirements of law. Men must be made to understand that the free consent of woman is a necessary precedent to sexuality; and if woman will be brave and firm, this can soon be brought about. She holds the whole matter in her hands. She has but to command and man to obey. Her sexual demands, from long restriction and inaction, and consequent demoralization, can be commanded sufficiently to wring the guarantee of freedom from man, who now holds it merely by legal power.

Women of America! Will you, can you, dare you begin this glorious work? Have you the courage, the strength, the virtue, the purity, the godliness to do this thing? I conjure you by the memory of your mothers who suffered and are now hovering over to inspire your souls; by the memory of your own sorrows and sufferings, and by those that your darling daughters after you will have to endure unless you strike the blow, to rise in open rebellion against this cursed, this thrice-damned slavery to which woman, from time immemorial, has been in bondage.

I know the task is a great one; but its prophecy is still greater. You will not be left to fight alone. Many men there are whose souls are in deep sympathy with you, who will join your standard as soon as you dare to raise it. Your allies shall be legion, and you shall go on conquering and to conquer until a blessed emancipation shall dawn for womankind, such as eye hath not seen nor heart conceived, in which no woman will ever even seem to be compelled to sell her body to any man for a permanent home, or for the means to procure a temporary one. And when you shall have gained this glorious victory, then shall come the possibility of another and a better saying of St. Paul: that the last enemy that shall be destroyed is death, for you will then be free to enter upon the search for the elixir of life with which to conquer death. There is an elixir of life that, when found, shall banish death; and there shall be no more death, since it, too, shall be wallowed up in victory. Then shall the redeemed souls of earth sing the gladsome song: "Oh, death! where is thy sting; oh grave, where is thy victory?"

The origin of human life is in the sexual unity of man and

woman. The continuation of human life must be sought for in the same, and it will there be found. Mark me well, for I mean what I say and say what I mean: In a perfected sexuality shall continuous life be found. A stream never dries up so long as the spring from whence it flows, sends forth its crystal waters. So also shall life not come to an end when its springs shall not cease to send forth the vitalized waters of life, that earth's otherwise weary children may drink and live.

And behold the most despised of all human things, that which has been held too obscene to be talked about except in the dark, will become the salvation of the world from sin and consequent death. The stone that the builders rejected shall become the head of the corner.

Then shall the resurrection come also. Then shall they, who have in ages past, cast off their mortal coils, be able to come again and resume them at will and clothe themselves with flesh; and thus, also, shall a spiritualized humanity be able at will to throw off and take on its material clothing, and the two worlds be once more and forever united.

Such to me, my brothers and sisters, is the sublime mission of Spiritualism, to be outwrought through the sexual emancipation of woman, and her return to self-ownership and to individualized existence. And may Heaven's choicest blessings make it come quickly.

CHAPTER 4

The Elixir of Life; or, Why Do We Die?
An Oration
Introduced by Michael W. Perry

Victoria Woodhull delivered the first speech in this book, "The Principles of Social Freedom" (Chapter 2), to the general public in New York City and (six weeks later) in Boston. Fitting her message to her audience, she offered reasons why her free love ideas were better for society than almost universally held views about sex and marriage.

The second and blunter speech, "The Scare-crows of Sexual Slavery" (Chapter 3), was delivered to a large audience of Spiritualists gathered in a resort town to escape the dreadful heat of a New England August. As her closing words suggest, she wanted Spiritualism to take as its "sublime mission" the "sexual emancipation of women" from Judeo-Christian beliefs that she repeatedly attacked as little more than "scare-crows" intended to frighten the uninformed.

In the century and more since that speech, a clash with two of the nation's most deeply imbedded religions has often signaled that a blend of eugenics and altered sexual behavior was being promoted. During eugenics first half century, new religions were advanced to supplant the old. Francis Galton, usually credited with founding modern eugenics, admitted as much when he gave three stages for getting a nation to adopt the ideology. The third was for eugenics to be "introduced into the national conscience, like a new religion."[1] For Woodhull, speaking almost thirty years, earlier, that religion was Spiritualism. For the famous Swedish feminist Ellen Key, it would come, "when the whole of humanity awakens to the consciousness of the 'holiness of generation.'"[2] For the sociologist Charlotte Perkins Gilman, it was the "Maternal Pantheism" in her serialized novel, *Herland* (1915).[3]

---

1. G. K. Chesterton, *Eugenics and Other Evils* (Seattle: Inkling Books, 2000), 130. The quote is in an appendix to the Inkling edition in a speech, "Eugenics: Its Definition, Scope, and Aims," that Francis Galton read to the Sociological Society in London on May 16, 1904.
2. Michael W. Perry, ed, *The Pivot of Civilization in Historical Perspective* (Seattle: Inkling Books, 2001), 65. Quoted from her *The Century of the Child* (1909).
3. Michael W. Perry, ed., *The Pivot of Civilization*, 125.

In this third speech, "The Elixir of Life," given just a month after her second speech, she is again speaking to Spiritualists, this time at their Tenth Annual Convention in Chicago. But now her message is much more deeply rooted in Spiritualism and in sexual mysticism. The result may seem odd to those who don't accept their beliefs.

"Spirits," Woodhull told her audience, that "have never deceived me," had informed her that "all the Planets in the Siderial [probably sidereal, an astronomical term] Universe are now congregated watching the issue of this momentous question; which must be solved rightly else the universe will go backward into a darkness from which it will require millions of years for it to emerge even to its present condition." (3)

What was that earthly issue on which the fate of the universe hinged? First, nowhere in the universe had the "inhabitants of even the oldest planets" acquired an ability to "put the last enemy—death—under foot." According to her, "disease, when the new era shall be inaugurated, will be banished from the human body." (5) This goes far beyond her earlier claim that free love would make women happier and result in fewer hungry children. For her, sex properly practiced is "The Elixir of Life"—nothing less than eternal life.

How would that marvelous transformation happen? According to her, "almost all disease among adults is caused by some unnatural or untimely sexual condition." (6) On the next page she drew a contrast between two situations. "Sexual intercourse that is in accordance with nature, and therefore proper, is that which is based upon mutual love and desire" (7) and brings good health. But, if sexual intercourse under other conditions, "be maintained for any considerable length of time, disease and sexual demoralization will surely follow." (7)

For Woodhull, the chief foe of healthy sex was marriage itself. "Modern marriage," she told her audience, creates "sexual slaves, who otherwise would be free." (8) But marriage, she went on to say, has a "graver consideration" (9) behind it. Children conceived within these almost universally unhappy marriages, bear "the mark of Cain upon their brows; or else with the seeds of some fatal disease in their systems; which accounts for one-half of them dying off before they reach the age of five years." (9) That ill-health, we will be told, is the result of their mother's unwilling acquisition to sex at the time of their conception.

Medically, what Woodhull was saying was nonsense. We have not eliminated marriage as she wanted, and yet the death rate for children has declined dramatically. We did it by eliminating the causes of diseases that were actually killing children in that era: polluted water, tainted food, and crowded living conditions.

But despite that glaring error, we should hear Woodhull out. It would be wrong to dismiss her entire system because of one mistake, however serious. She was trying to turn her sister's "What will become of the children if marriage be done away?" argument upside down, not by merely claiming that without marriage things will get no worse, but by claiming that sex within marriage itself was the cause of most social ills. This is Woodhull at her most radical position about free love.

Marriage does often result in women being economically dependent on men. But rather than regarding that as a necessary result of the great effort required to rear children, Woodhull saw it a problem. Using arguments still echoed today, for her women have been reduced to "sexual slaves," (8) trading undesired sex for economic support, with the result that it is "impossible for a woman to remain in health under unnatural sexual conditions, as it is for a person to take poison and not suffer from its effects." (8) The result is the "demoralized and degenerate condition of female humanity." (9) Ironically, although blasted as a sexual libertine, what Woodhull was saying probably appealed most strongly to those frigid women who are said to be common during the Victorian era.

To solve the problem, Woodhull wanted women to become "independent of the individual man for support." (9) No longer husbands and fathers, men are to become little more than free-floating sperm donors, supporting children they hardly know through their taxes. (We might ask if that sort of life is healthy for men.) As a result, women, no longer forced to trade sex for financial support, will have only what we might call 'happy sex' and produce healthy children.

Woodhull was thinking too narrowly, focusing only on money. Even when financially independent, women may still find themselves giving sex to get a man's attention, however brief. By linking an enduring relationship to a variety of things men may find appealing, including fatherhood and companionship, marriage does much more for women than a monthly check from the government can ever do. Woodhull did not see things that way. Without marriage and no longer needing a husband's support, she claimed, not only would "no unwelcomed children born," (9) but children will be "born in health and with a lease on life beyond the adult age." (9) Here we see the disease and death-free lives that Woodhull promised earlier, as well as some of her earliest and least scientific ideas about eugenics.

Woodhull did not forget environmental influences. According to her the children of this fleeting 'happy sex,' no longer dependent on the money-making abilities of now-absent fathers, "will all inherit the same right to equal education... and thus enter upon adult life having had equal preparation." (9) That's the Brave New World's "Hatchery and Conditioning Centre" we discussed in the previous chapter, with some forty-five children assigned to a rotating series of mother-surrogates who indoctrinate all their charges to a single point of view unhindered by a father or mother. Woodhull would not be the last to equate egalitarian sameness with social good, even when that sameness was dreadful.

Her idea is obviously flawed. Even assuming that you create a world in which all babies are conceived as a result of "mutual love and desire," however brief, what is link between a woman's desiring sex one night and her attitude toward nine months of pregnancy and perhaps a year of nursing? Happy sex is not the same as happy motherhood.

It's also hard to imagine a happy mother giving up her year-old child to a host of indifferent surrogate mothers, much less to a State-run indoctrination program, however much it might promise to be egalitarian and scientific. Many women want children not because they enjoy the pregnancy or the insistent demands of a newborn, but because they look forward to having a more mature son or daughter to enjoy as an equal. Yet, as we will see, Woodhull would take away the best, leaving only the most difficult part of parenting—the messy diapers—and claim that the result would be "no unwelcome children born." Strange!

Stripped of its unrealistic psychology and the mysticism of watching spirits living other worlds, there was something concrete behind what she was saying. Woodhull believed in a ruthless form of "it takes a village to rear a child." She believed that the State would do better at rearing healthy children than married parents. She said precisely that.

To begin. Children must first be conceived, gestated, and born in proper conditions; and afterward, properly and scientifically reared and educated; and with this neither marriage or present customs will have aught to do; indeed they have nothing to do with such matters now, except to interpose obstacles in the way of their natural development. People argue as if children are the result of marriage, while the truth is that to them, marriage is an arbitrary incident, merely, entailing unthought of misery. (10)

Having provided what she thought was a superior form of child rearing, Woodhull then stepped back to explain why children born under her scheme will be superior in endowment as well as environment. She asks how "children begotten under the rule of love and consent, can possibly be bad?" (11)—as if the mother's feelings at the time of conception determined everything. Her own "theory of stirpiculture," (11) a term then used for eugenics, denied that possibility. The key to the "best child" a woman could produce, she said, lay in finding the man that the woman "loves and for whom she has the keenest sexual desire." Woodhull went on to hope that, "nobody will hereafter class me among those stirpiculturists, who reduce the begetting of children to the level of that of cattle; and who would exalt the best merely physically endowed men to be the progenitors of the race, without regard to any natural attraction and denying sexuality to all of inferior endowment." That's certainly true. Some eugenic schemes do leave the impression that anything less than a stud farm compromised eugenic principles. Maintaining the population might dictate that perhaps half of all women have children simply because wombs are a limited resource, but it did not require that more than a small number of superiorly endowed men become fathers.

But Woodhull left herself wiggling room with that last remark. The real issue in stirpiculture and eugenics was not "denying sexuality to all of inferior endowment" but denying parenthood. If then-popular beliefs about prenatal influences on a mother affecting the child began to fade and science became more aware of the role of inheritance (as it would), then Woodhull could easily change her means, abandoning romantically inspired free love for more scientific measures, in order to achieve her goal—a society having only healthy, long-lived children. That theme in Woodhull's thinking is explored in more detail in the companion volume, *Lady Eugenist*. Here we look at Woodhull's earlier ideas (*circa* 1873), when eugenics as sexual mysticism argued in favor of a free love, with free love being regarded as the more important. That attitude perhaps still reflected the priorities of the sex-obsessed male founders of some of the utopian communities of the 1840s and 1850s.

Later, Woodhull would adopt an agenda more common among feminists whose beliefs were not rooted in utopian cults or Spiritualism, beliefs in which eugenics trumps free love and sex for the 'unfit' can only take place when there are technological means—birth control, sterilization and abortion—to prevent unwanted births. However, given the limited reliability and safety of those technologies in the late nineteenth century, the eugenics Woodhull promoted then was only practical if allegedly inferior women avoided both sex and marriage, a most unrealistic situation, and if all seriously 'unfit' women were confined to single-sex institutions during their reproductive years, something that was very costly. (That explains her later zeal for forced sterilization.)

In the end, much of what Woodhull said in this speech had no staying power. It was too weird and too mystical. While rhetoric about a 'wanted child' continues, in today's more covert forms of eugenics, no one claims that merely wanting sex or a child causes that child to be born with a superior endowment. Now, at least among the self-appointed experts, all that we are or will be is dictated by a blend of heredity and environment. Control that, and they think they control us and the society around us. That's the fundamental flaw with all such thinking.

What passed from the (early) Woodhull of this book to the (later) Woodhull of *Lady Eugenist*, and what would be taken up by others, is the very opposite of "individual personal freedom, culminating in perfect sexual liberty." (24) It is the belief that breeding and child rearing lie within the domain of the State. To make that more appealing, today it is often be linked to offers of State-sanctioned sexual license that even Woodhull might have found disturbing. The result—a sexual wasteland of fatherless, emotionally scarred children whose mothers have their economic independence from men provided by a monthly welfare check—has so little to do with what she once praised as "a pearl of great price" and "the world's redemption," (24) that, were she alive today, we might hope she would attack the failures of at least that portion of her own legacy. But maybe not.

THE

ELIXIR OF LIFE;

OR,

WHY DO WE DIE?

AN ORATION

DELIVERED BEFORE THE

TENTH ANNUAL CONVENTION

OF THE

AMERICAN ASSOCIATION OF SPIRITUALISTS,

AT

Grow's Opera House, Chicago, Ills.,

BY

VICTORIA C. WOODHULL,

SEPTEMBER 18, 1873.

———•———

New York:
WOODHULL & CLAFLIN.
1873.

The Elixir of Life; or, Why Do We Die?

I appear before you to-night to speak of a subject which, more than any other, ought to command the attention of the enlightened world ; but which, more than any other, receives the anathemas of ist professed representatives—the so-called Christians—because, forsooth, to discuss it, is to attack, necessarily, one of the chiefest pillars of the Christian edifice. The subject involves the necessity of free speech, in plain terms. John Stuart Mill, whom all reformers have learned to love, said : "The diseases of society can, no more than corporeal maladies, be prevented or cured, without being spoken about in plain language." I propose to speak about the diseases of society, and if I expect to present either a preventative or a cure, I must speak in terms so plain that none can mistake my meaning. You may affect to blush, and the papers may call me indecent and vulgar, and say I have no shame, to speak as I shall, what they do not dare to repeat. But ought not you and they rather blush with shame that such diseases as I shall mention, exist at all to be spoken about ? I say shame upon the newspapers, and shame upon your preachers, teachers and doctors, that I should have cause to stand here and tell you what they should have freely discussed, years ago, and thus have saved me the present unpleasant task.

Standing, however, as I do, somewhat representative of the immense issue of sexual freedom that is now agitating the public mind, I have a duty to fulfill, to which I should be recreant did I withhold a single sentence that I propose to utter. But, more than this, even : I am intrusted with a mission by those whose disapproval I would not earn, were it to gain the approval of a thousand audiences like this ; therefore, though the task be not a pleasant one, I would not shirk it if I could. If, however, in performing it, instead of driving you farther away from me than you now are, I should draw you all nearer, then should I indeed thank heaven for giving me the moral strength to utter the plain, unvarnished truth, as I know it, about the most important question that has ever interested or distracted the human mind.

I ask you for the time being, to cast aside your prejudices; to unloose every fetter that hangs about your minds ; to disperse all clouds that shadow your understanding, and to not prejudge me by concluding in advance that you know more about this matter than I do ; but let the words that I shall utter sink deep into your souls, since, some day, whether you heed them now or not, you will have cause to remember them. I ought to know more of what I am to speak about than almost any of you, because I have given it more attention ; but if there be any here who have studied it, in its various phases, one-half as deeply as I have, they will, with one possible exception, agree with me in everything that I shall say.

Still further in preparation, I wish to ask : Are there any here who fear the truth ? I hear no replies. Now again, are there any who are afraid of an error. Again I hear no replies. So if you are afraid neither of truth or error, I see no reason why you should quarrel with me about anything that I may advance ; since whatever it may be, it must be one of these. But I can tell you of what you are afraid—if, indeed, you are fearful at all. You are afraid that I may hold up a glass in which you will see your secret deformities ; and you scarcely dare to look upon them. But no matter. Let them be ever so hideous—and that they are hideous enough, I know right well—it will do you good to see yourselves, for once, as others see you. For there are those to whom your every thought and your most secret acts are as well known as they are to yourselves ; and let me remind you that, if your secrets were as well known to human beings as they are to spirits, none of you would be any the worse off, while many would thank heaven that they no longer carry the awful load alone. Hence it is of your own lives that you are afraid rather than of the truth : since he or she whom the truth will not stab, has no cause for fear.

I think I know enough of the world at large, and of individuals specially to say, that there are not a half dozen persons present, who are not in the most abject slavery to what the world pleases to call, their secret vices. Wouldn't it be strange if these should, after all, turn out to be virtues instead. Then wouldn't their subjects be heartily ashamed of themselves for having been frightened at shadows, merely, into being liars, thieves and hypocrites so large a part of their lives !

Again and finally, let me entreat that, for once in your lives, you throw off the sickly sentimentalism about sexual love—your sham morality and mock modesty about the most common and harmless, as well as innocent and beautiful of things ; and like common-sense individuals, with me, consider, specially, that department of our natures with which, though you have pretended such immaculateness, you would no sooner part than with life itself : indeed, to blot which out of life, would be to leave but a precious little worth living. For once be men and women, acting as if you were known by each other, as you are, to be men and women, possessed of all the endowments of nature, and wanting to know if there is still something to learn that will make them yet richer, more beautiful and bountiful of happiness than ever before ; and willing to accept the lesson at least for consideration, to which I will proceed without further delay.

I have said that this problem of sexual love is the most important one that ever engaged the human mind. It becomes so because within it is concealed the science that shall finally solve the problem of life and death, which must remain unsolved until this science is discovered to the world. When I say life and death, I mean literally what I say. I mean that within the sexual problem is concealed the law that shall enable us to solve the mystery of life by conquering death.

Immense as is this to the inhabitants of earth, how immeasurably more so shall it become when it is known that, upon this planet for the first time since creation, has this problem nearly approached a solution. Planets countless millions of ages older than this, have all their weary lengths run out, waiting for the fresh, green earth to give them the knowledge of life and death, that shall make them superior to both.

The resurrection of the body, and the ascension, at will, of the Spirit have never been attained by the inhabitants of even the oldest planets. These, although immensely superior to the people of the earth, in physical, intellectual and moral culture, are less advanced than we are, as a people, spiritually. This fact has come to be known to the inhabitants of the solar system, and their attention is now centered upon this planet in hopeful anticipation, willing, in order to obtain the prize, to yield to us the palm. Here, then, the palm must be won. Here, death must be conquered. Here must be produced to the wailing Universe, the individuality, the personality, that has partaken of the Elixir of Life, and thereby put the last enemy—death—under foot. And here it will be done, and the glad anthem ring out upon the startled world, "Oh, death where is thy sting! Oh, grave where is thy victory!"

Do you ask me how I know this? I will tell you. Spirits, who have never deceived me, have informed and shown me why it must be so; and I know from the intense anxiety now existing among the Spirits, to whom this solution has been intrusted, that they feel a responsibility about it resting upon them, such as was never before borne by either mortals or Spirits. They tell me that Spirits from all the Planets in the Siderial Universe are now congregated; watching the issue of this momentous question, which must be solved rightly, else the universe will go backward into a darkness from which it will require millions of years for it to emerge even to its present condition.

That which has been undergoing the process of evolution since the birth of the first planet, is now at the culminating point. The efforts of the various epochs have centered to evolve a new and higher order of life, in which the wants and requirements of the purely physical existence, and the consequent demoralization and dishonesty that have crept into the world, through them, shall be done away with. The whole power of the great and good of the boundless universe is stretched to the utmost tention to attain it. If it shall succeed; if it shall reach the culmination; if the gladsome song of victory shall sound out upon the world, even though it be from a lowly manger, and from a despised Nazarene, civilization will spring forward by a single bound, a million years in advance of the present period.

But if it fail—I shudder as I contemplate the possibility. Nothing that has ever occurred to the world; nothing that the Millerites have ever believed; nothing that has ever been pictured of despair and darkness, can, for a moment, compare with that prospect. You look back almost with horror, to the dark ages that followed the submersion of civilization, when the forests of the North of Europe poured down their Goths and Vandals and Huns upon the devoted city of Rome. This was but the result of a physical contest over a physical civilization. Then how much more horrible must be the fate, that would follow the defeat in a Spiritual contest, in which the prize to be gained or lost is Spiritual life. The Barbarians of Europe succeeded in the former contest; now after a thousand years, let it not be said that the barbarians of earth have again triumphed; and this time over, not only the highest civilization of earth, but over this, reinforced by the armies of heaven. Let it not be said, that flaming hells yawn again; that tormenting fiends are again set free; that cloven-footed devils are again unloosed for "a thousand years," since if they conquer they will reign inexorably. A fearful tragedy or a glorious victory await us; and upon us here assembled perhaps depends the momentous issue.

Do not, however, receive this as coming from me; but accept it as coming from the wisest and best of ascended Spirits—those whom you have learned to honor and love for the good done while on the earthly plane; those to whom, if they were to appear before you here, you would willingly yield implicit obedience; and who would appear here, were not the one essential element still wanting, and to whom for six years I have yielded a willing and appreciative obedience. Gladly would I name them. They are familiar to you all; but I must not presume beyond my commission; but I am commissioned, aye commanded, to declare unto you, and through you to the world, that in the despised, the ignored problem of Sexuality, lies the key that shall unlock to Spirits the doors of materiality, and show in boldest relief that of which, the most blessed, have as yet caught but faintest glimpses—Spirit Materialization.

The perfected blending of the positive and negative creative forces, which has never yet been accomplished, must furnish the special elements, now needed, to perfect and make general the possibility of spirit resurrection. Of course I cannot offer you the proofs of this. It is something of which as yet there is no proof. During the past eighteen months, thousands of persons have been put on trial, as the means to present this to the world, and I know there are a few, at least, here present, to whom this prophecy has been made; but alas all have failed, and the whole power of the spirit world is now centered upon a single individual to effect it, and all the opposing powers of hell and darkness are also centered upon the same individual to defeat it.

I know these things, and fearful to me have been the means by which this knowledge came. So terrible at times have they been that I have shrunk affrighted from the contemplation. For months I lacked the courage to launch this question upon the world; for months again I lacked the courage to do that which has called the world to the discussion of the social problem; and still again for months have I hesitated to do what I am doing to-night; but the exigency is such that it could be delayed no longer, although some of the necessary elements are lacking still. The law must be advanced, though the illustrations be delayed.

Shall I now proclaim what it is that is wanting to complete the victory; that which will once and forever settle this question of sexuality, and from this mud-bedaubed, filth-defiled, Christian-damned, this vulgar, indecent, and obscene thing, which Christianity has made it out to be, lift it to rest upon the brow of every man and woman, as the chiefest jewel in their crown of brilliants? Will you now permit me, in the name of the spirit-world, to proclaim what it is that is wanting to accomplish this—a greater, grander, a more pregnant for good revolution, than all others that have preceded it?

But first let me explain what the results of all this will be—what fearful existing social diseases are to be changed and cured—so that, from their possibility, together with their desirability, as the greatest of human needs, you may the more readily consider the means by which they must come, if they come at all. I urge you to consider them in the true spirit of inquiry, confessing that you have not yet arrived at infinite truth, and conjuring you to accept truth, in whatever garb or form it appears, even if it be revolutionary to every present thought and action in the world.

Not anybody will deny the desirability of a perfected physical health for humanity ; but many may doubt the possibility of its attainment. I, however, make the bold, bald assertion, that disease, when the new era shall be inaugurated, will be banished the human body ; and that too by the same means that shall make the era a new one. Almost everybody has witnessed the beneficent results of so-called magnetism in the removal of disease ; as well as the further fact that not the same magnetism will produce equally beneficial results upon the same disease in different persons ; and still further, that magnetic effects are the most positive and apparent when the operator and subject are of different sexes. It has also been observed that these effects may be produced, though distance separate the persons involved ; but that the effects are more palpable when they are, for instance, in the same room, with their minds concentrated upon the conditions ; and still more so, when there is actual physical contact over the parts diseased.

Now what is the philosophy of this healing by magnetic power? This, simply, and it has a whole volume of meaning in it, to the analytic observer: That the operator and the subject, are positively and negatively related to each other; that the approach of the poles of the battery have been sufficiently near to make the connection, and that upon the perfectness of the connection depends the extent of the effect produced, and the consequent curative influence. That is to say, where a person positive or negative to another, afflicted with disease, is brought into magnetic relations, with this other, and the positive and negative currents are established, that disease, whatever it may be, necessarily departs, since where these currents exist, disease cannot remain.

It is safe then to assume that all diseases that have not already destroyed organs upon which life depends may and ought to be cured; and, if this method of cure were once established, no disease would be permitted to go on to the extent of vital organic destruction, and conquently that death from disease would be virtually abolished.

This is the philosophy; but upon what is this philosophy based? What is this magnetic relation that produces such wonderful results? It is called Animal Magnetism, and so indeed it is. But what is Animal Magnetism? It is Sexual vitality merely; and it is nothing else. A person, whether male or female, cannot be a magnetic healer, except he have sexual vitality; and it will be found, that the most successful healers, are those who have the most of this element. Nor does the fact that those of the same sex, often relieve each other, impeach this statement; since he who has the vitality, imparts it to him who hath it not, by the law of equalization.

It is an axiom in the medical profession that the patient who experiences sexual desire is not dangerously ill; and also that the patient who has been dangerously ill is convalescent when sexual desire returns. Thus, it is held that the presence of the sexual appetite is a symptom of health; but if it turn out, as I hold that it will, this statement, to make it strictly true, will have to be reversed. That is, cause and effect have been transposed, the effect having been placed behind the cause. Sexual appetite is the basis of health, and when re-established in an invalid, health follows. This becomes clear, when it is considered upon what a cure by magnetism depends. It is the restoration of sexual vitality, or animal magnetism—the introduction of this into the system of the patient, causing health; and not a certain condition of health, making it possible for it to be introduced. Thus in this as in almost all pretended science, the real truth reverses the existing order of things; and in this if what I say be true, you will see how nearly the whole world is bordering on promiscuous sexual intercourse, and not only this, but how much the health and happiness of the world depend upon still further, so-called promiscuousness, or, more strictly, perhaps, upon a harmonious variety or a composite and a perfected unity.

But this may not be so evident until another fact is made clear. And this fact is this: almost all disease among adults is caused by some unnatural or untimely sexual condition. Take the married classes. Show me a man or woman who is a picture of physical health and strength, and I will show you a person, who has healthy sexual relations; but these may be at the expense of the other person in the partnership. Show me, however, a man and a woman who live together, who are perfectly healthy, physically, and I will show you a God-ordained marriage, which man cannot put asunder. Or again, show me men and women who are in perfect health, whether they are married according to law, or whether they live monogamically or promiscuously, and I will show you persons who are living according to the laws of nature, sexually, and, consequently, are living rightly. Dispute this who can!

It is useless to kick against facts. They are stubborn things, and the world has been butting its head against the science and facts of sexuality, already too long. Although the attempt has been made to bury it in the mud, it shall, nevertheless, be exalted white and pure, to the throne; and there it shall rule the world in peace, happiness and endless progress. If, as I tell you the fountain of health, is concealed in this great problem, shall we be so foolish as to longer ignore it, and thus deprive ourselves of its priceless boon? I say, No! A thousand times, No! Rather let every thing that is held sacred or profane, perish in a common ruin, than let this problem remain longer unsolved.

If health depend upon proper sexuality, it follows that disease depends upon improper sexuality. To this general proposition I make another and a specific one: That all disease not directly to be attributed to so-called accidental causes, is the result of improper, or the want of proper, sexual conditions. And this applies to persons of all ages and both sexes. Show me the man or woman, married or single, old or young, who is suffering from any chronic complaint, and I will show you a person who has either improper or no sexual relations.

Now, just here arises the great and grave question: What are and what are not proper sexual relations. In endeavoring to answer this, I must be permitted to speak so as to be properly understood. And why should I not? Are we not endowed by nature with the sexual passion; and is it not given us for a purpose—one that should be a blessing, instead of a curse as it mostly is, to humanity? Nobody will pretend to answer, No! Then why should we not discuss it as freely as we do any other subject? Is it because our thoughts and desires about it have become so abominable, so perverted and so impure, obscene and vulgar, that any, even needed reference to the subject, brings the blush of shame to the face and a sense of degradation to the soul? Are we indeed so impure that to us all sexual things are impure? I lay it down as an axiom that he or she who blushes and is ashamed at any mention of sexual intercourse, has, at some time or other, done something sexually of which to be ashamed. I hold that every thing connected with the manner and method in which human life has its fountain, is a proper and a modest subject for either public or private discussion, and I simply pity all who say Nay! to this.

Sexual intercourse that is in accordance with nature, and therefore proper, is that which is based upon mutual love and desire, and that ultimates in reciprocal benefit. Sexual intercourse that is improper is that which is not based upon mutual love and desire, and that does not ultimate in reciprocal benefit. Of the former there is but one class of cases, since in this class, all the conditions of perfectness are present. First, Love; Second, desire based upon love ; and, Third, mutual happiness as the result. Who is there that shall dare to interfere with such sexual relations? Let it be whoever it may, he is an impious wretch, and an enemy to human happiness, and consequently to humanity.

Of the latter there are several classes, which deserve to be enumerated, so that they may be understood wherever any of them may be met. First, that class where it is claimed by legal right ; second, that class where the female, to please the male, submits without the proper self desire ; third, that class where, for money, or any motive other than love, the female sells the use of her body to the male for his gratification ; fourth, that class where mutual love and desire exist, but where there is such want of adaptation as to make mutual consummation impossible.

Now, under either of these conditions, if sexual intercourse be maintained for any considerable length of time, disease and sexual demoralization will surely follow; but the most destructive to health as well as the most numerous, are the first and the last classes, which occur almost altogether in marriage. The wife who submits to sexual intercourse against her wishes or desires, virtually commits suicide; while the husband who compels it, commits murder, and ought just as much to be punished for it, as though he strangled her to death for refusing him.

But this even is not so destructive to health as is that intercourse, carried on habitually, without regard to perfect and reciprocal consummation. And when it is known that three-fourths of all married women, who otherwise might be happily mated, suffer from this cause, the terrible and wide-spread results may be readily conceived, and the need for amelioration as readily understood. I need not explain to any woman the effects of unconsummated intercourse though she may attempt to deceive herself about it; but every man needs to have it thundered in his ears until he wakes to the fact that he is not the only party to the act, and that the other party demands a return for all that he receives; demands that he shall not be enriched at her expense; demands that he shall not, either from ignorance or selfish desire, carry her impulse forward on its mission only to cast it backward with the mission unfulfilled, to prostrate the impelling power and to breed nervous debility or irritability and sexual demoralization, and to sow the seeds of disease broadcast among humanity. What is merely hinted at here involves a whole science and a fine art, incomparably the most important of all the sciences and of all the arts, hardly yet broached to the human thought, and now criminally repressed and defeated in their effort at birth by the prejudices of mankind—by your prejudices, and even, perhaps, by mine.

It is a fact terrible to contemplate, yet it is nevertheless true, and ought to be pressed upon the world for its recognition: that fully one-half of all women seldom or never experience any pleasure whatever in the sexual act. Now this is an impeachment of nature, a disgrace to our civilization—an eternal blotch upon the otherwise chivalrous conduct of men toward women. It is a standing reproach upon physiological science that this ignorance has existed so long; and upon medical science, that its dire effects have been so long concealed. I have recently had repeated interviews with a member, in high standing, of the New York College of Physicians; and he does not hesitate to acknowledge that, more than all I have yet said is true, about the sexual demoralization of the race; but the age of hypocrisy reigns as supremely in this, as in the clerical profession. Its members are waiting for the world to get ready to hear the truth, and have thus made it necessary that a weak woman should proclaim it, who, instead of being a recognized authority, competent to enforce her statements, is almost crucified, because she feels it her duty to do what they should have done, whose business it is to guard the health of humanity.

Now it is as impossible for a woman to remain in health under unnatural sexual conditions, as it is for a person to take poison and not suffer from its effects; and every woman who hears me knows this is true. They know that the demoralized and degenerate condition of female humanity is to be attributed to false sexual relations; but who among them have the courage to declare it? I have had hundreds of wives say to me, "I would not endure these conditions a single moment, were I not dependent upon my husband for a home," or "if society would not ostracize me for leaving him;" or some other equally lamentable excuses. To these my reply has been, "You have the face to tell me this, and almost in the same moment you shrug your shoulders at a passing prostitute whose features beam with health, and whose rounded form speaks of unmistakable strength and beauty, while your face and form are a living condemnation of your life, let it be what it may."

Out upon such damned hypocrisy. "I hold that the poor woman, who, cast out by society, because, in ignorance, she admitted her lover, without procuring a license, to the sacred relations of love, is compelled to sell her body to some demanding man, for the pitiful means to keep life in her body, and perhaps in that of her unrecognized child, is as high as heaven above her who, in silks and satins and with a long retinue of friends, and the sanction of the priest and the law, marries a home for life, with a repugnance in her soul for the man who furnishes it.

I can have a deep sympathy and respect for the modest prostitute who feels the degradation into which she is almost compelled by the ostracism of society ; but for her who goes through the gorgeous pageantry of a modern marriage, to proclaim to the world that she is now going to enter into sexual relations with the man, with whom she has consorted, every other way, for an indefinite time, according to the recognized standard of sexual things, I can regard only as brazen and immodest. To me this farce of marriage is a public placarding, merely, to this effect: that I, the bearer, am this day sold, to be the sexual slave of the person to whom the law, holding that I do not know enough and am unable to protect myself, has committed the care of my person. Wives may not think they are slaves, and yet be open to this charge. Some may not be ; but let the large majority attempt to assert their sexual freedom, and they will quickly come to the realization.

To what does modern marriage amount, if it be not to hold sexual slaves, who otherwise would be free? I ask the married : Do you live together because the law compels you? And they scout the idea; but in the same breath they condemn me for saying that the law only binds people who ought to be set free, and who, without the law, would be free: that those whom God—Love—has bound together no man, or woman, can put asunder.

Beside the evils of improper sexual relations resulting from legalized prostitution, there are the still more terrific conditions to which they are condemned, who languish in single cursedness. To this very considerable portion of female humanity the right to the exercise and enjoyment of their sexual instincts is absolutely denied, under the penalty of social death. They are condemned to a life of degradation and misery, from which there is no escape. Add to this class who are sexually starved, those who are compelled to undesired relations with the legal owners of their sexual organs, and a sum total of misery is formed which altogether beggars description.

I have not the inclination to go through with the sickening details that have come into my possession, in my investigation into this subject. Suffice it to say, that I know fully one-half of the world is undergoing sexual starvation; dying either for the want of intercourse, or for lack of the proper kind.

There is, however, another and a graver consideration lying back of the present demoralized sexual condition of the people; and this is the result it is producing upon the coming generation. If the present social system of compulsory marriage were all that its admirers claim for it; were it the guardian of peace, prosperity and purity; in short, were it the one thing good and true in our present civilization, yet for the curse it entails upon children, I would wash it out, if need be, by the blood of one-half of our race.

Four-fifths of all children who are conceived are undesired, and they come into the world, as it were, with the brand of Cain upon their brows; or else with the seeds of some fatal disease in their systems; which accounts for one-half of them dying off before they reach the age of five years—a commentary upon the present social system that sinks it to the level of a horrid, aye, a brutal tragedy. And yet the world pretends to have a deep solicitude for the children. It crieth out: What will become of the children if marriage be done away?

I will tell you just what will become of the children, which, if the children of to-day had inherited, I should not now have had occasion to enter my protest against the awful crime, that is being committed against them. In the first place, without marriage, and with women made, as they must be, independent of the individual man for support, there will be no unwelcomed children born; secondly, they will be born in health and with a lease of life beyond the adult age, and, thirdly, they will all inherit the same right to equal education—physical, mental and moral, and thus enter upon adult life having had equal preparation.

It is as much better to be the ward of society than to be dependent upon an individual, as society is greater than the individual. Who would not rather have the bond of the United States—even under present political conditions—than that of any individual? How much more to be preferred for children, then, will be the faith of the future reconstructed government, over either the legal or moral duty of the individual merely. They would do well to examine the outcome of children, who cry out against the social revolution, because of them. Of all the improved conditions possible, those of dependent women and children will be most improved. We are looking earnestly forward to a better race of men and women, and one of the means by which it will be produced, will be this condition for children.

To begin. Children must first be conceived, gestated and born in proper conditions ; and afterward, properly and scientifically reared and educated ; and with *this neither marriage or present customs* will have aught to do ; indeed they have nothing to do with such matters now, except to interpose obstacles in the way of their natural development. People argue as if children are the result of marriage, while the truth is, that to them, marriage is an arbitrary incident, merely, entailing unthought of misery.

It is also to be observed that another horrible result of the system of marriage, is sexual vice, both in children and adults, and when its terrific ravages are considered, a remedy, let it be whatever it may, should be joyfully welcomed by the whole world. I need not tell you that four-fifths of the children practice self-abuse before they are old enough, of their own wisdom to know better ; nor that, finding the inroads it is making upon their health, they attempt to abandon it, and spermatorrhea is substituted for the original vice ; nor that almost everybody, female as well as male, when licensed, legally, to enter upon the relations of sex, are so fearfully debilitated by this vice, or this disease, as to debar them from even a medium measure of happiness ; and still more to unfit them to reproduce themselves in children. Indeed does vice in childhood culminate i misery in adult life !

The repressions of law and a pretended public opinion, and the resulting enforced and unwilling relations in marriage, are already yielding their natural fruit—a growing disgust sexually, between the sexes. Were I to tell you the extent to which Sodomy in man and its antitype in woman have attained, I should shock you beyond measure ; and if to this I were to add the beastly practices to which resort is had to revive or stimulate the depraved and demoralized sexuality in men, and women too, I should disgust you, though speaking nothing but the truth, and such-truth as the world needs to know.

I am only reiterating what is known to be true, by those who have investigated the subject, medically and physiologically, when I say that a change for the better must soon be made ; since if things go on for the next century as they have for the last, there will be no further reproduction possible, or even desirable. These are questions of mighty import for the consideration of the present. They come to *us*, and *we* must determine whether the race shall become extinct, or whether we will have the moral courage to inquire into the matter. and find the remedy ; and when found to apply it.

For my part I do not care what that remedy may be. I do not care if it be promiscuous sexual intercourse for both sexes and all ages. I do not care if it be, what is to me, the most unpalatable of things. I would gladly seize hold of it, and expend every possible effort to secure its inauguration.

But when the remedy shall be found and accepted, it will be in perfect harmony with the highest happiness and conditions, and the best interests possible for humanity. It cannot be promiscuous sexuality ; since I am prepared to prove that a person who follows this, becomes impotent in from six to ten years. And yet I am charged with advocating such a thing as this. Perhaps, however, we do not yet fully understand what promiscuous sexuality really is Promiscuousness signifies without selection or choice; it means indiscriminately. Harmonious and reciprocal variety is not, in any proper sense, promiscuousness; nor does it lead to the effect of promiscuousness, which, as I said before, is impotency.

Indeed if I were to sum up the meaning of the movement for sexual freedom in a single sentence, I should say : It is a strife for supremacy between bestiality in sexual intercourse, on the one hand, and its normal expression, according to the law of its own nature, on the other hand. And opponents shall not escape that point, nor blind the eyes of the ignorant, nor even rouse the superstition of the vulgar, much longer, by the cry of promiscuousness, when in this strife we know that promiscuousness shall go down in a common ruin with everything else in sexuality that has brought misery, desolation and death into the world.

Now, the remedy for all the ills to which I have called your attention is the substitution for the present rule of sexual intercourse, the rule of mutual consent based upon mutual desire, which may be temporary, or may continue during life. To prove this, permit me to ask if any person ever knew of any detrimental results following from the application of that rule ; did ever any disease, or anything but happiness and peace, follow from natural, mutually desired sexuality? I tell you nay ! You may search the world through and through and fail to find a single exception. It is impossible that anything but good should follow the natural expression of a natural desire ; while we have found that almost all the ills of life, follow as the results of intercourse, based upon an entirely opposite rule.

Again, let me ask if any body is so blind as to imagine that the law has anything whatever to do with the begetting of good children ; and again, if children begotten under the rule of love and consent, can possibly be bad?

And here I desire to correct an error that exists regarding my theory of stirpiculture. It is supposed by many, that I contend, when a woman desires a child she should select for its parent, some person, who, from physical health and perfectness, should be something like an ideal man. I utterly repudiate all such stirpiculture as this. I do not believe it possible for a woman to produce her best child, except by the man whom she loves best and for whom she has the keenest sexual desire. If this be for the perfect physical man, why, all the better ; but I have observed that even when the physical conditions of parents are not so good as they ought to be, but when they are closely allied by love, that good children follow ; while I have seen the most inferior children result from parents who, from physical appearances, ought, apparently, to beget the very best ; therefore I am obliged to conclude that the order of children depends not so much upon the physical perfection of parents, as it does upon the perfectness of the love upon which the sexual impulse is based, that precedes conception. The conditions for the future generation of children, then, are : 1st, Perfect love ; 2d, Mutual desire ; 3d, Perfect health.

Furthermore, I hold that for a woman to have sexual intercourse with a man, for any other reason than that she loves him and has a sexual desire for him, is to degrade herself, while the opposite conditions must always produce the opposite effect of exaltation. I hope, therefore, that nobody will hereafter class me among those stirpiculturists, who reduce the begetting of children to the level of that of cattle; and who would exalt the best merely physically endowed men to be the progenitors of the race, without regard to any natural attraction and denying sexuality to all of inferior endowments. I repeat again, and I wish emphatically to impress it upon you, that, to me, love is the element by which the best children are begotten; and that when there shall be no sexual intercourse except that based upon love, then there will be no half-made-up children born to be a curse to themselves, and a burden to society.

Again it is to be observed that there it no course so safe when there is danger of any kind ahead, as to have those who are to encounter it fully informed of its character, and thus prepared to meet it. But in the matter of sexuality, the world's practice is entirely different. Those who know anything about the dangers by which the sexual passion is surrounded, make the most strenuous efforts to conceal them from those who are ignorant of the perils which attend their development. It is utterly incomprehensible to me how mothers, fathers, teachers, preachers and doctors are so diligent in impressing the young under their charges against the habits of lying, cheating and stealing, while never a word is said to them about the dangers of self abuse. Children at some period of growth find a strange sensation present with them, and in their simplicity, perhaps, seek to learn what it all means; but they are met with a certain and effectual rebuff, and probably are treated to a dissertation about the awful wickedness of such thoughts, and the most positive injunction never again to entertain them. But they will come, and they will not be discarded, and thus they are left to drift almost assuredly into obtaining, surreptitiously, sufficient knowledge to teach them the manner in which gratification is had. With this knowledge, added to the stifled but still growing passion, they decline into a morbid sexual condition which, running into years, carries them beyond the possibility of a return to natural and healthy action and to maturity, utterly ruined, sexually and physically.

Now, in place of this repression, children need early instruction in the uses and abuses of sexuality. They need to be taught that it is a divinely-gifted agent for human happiness, and to regard it as a capacity to be cherished equally with all other capacities. All secretiveness and false modesty and sickly sentimentalism ought to be removed, and the subject reduced to an every-day affair, and thus we shall rob it of the morbidness and mawkishness by which it is now enveloped, and by which it is cursed, and the passion itself will be permitted to develop, healthfully, under the guidance of an enlightened understanding of all its possibilities.

From the day that sexual science is introduced into schools, as assuredly it will be, from that day the sexual evils that now beset the youth of both sexes will begin to vanish. Familiarity with anything robs it of the power to harm as well as of the power to demoralize. If this question of sex were as common a subject for conversation as that of diet or any other human need, many of the ills that now grow out of it would fade away, and it would be rapidly reduced to a science, and everybody come to know to whom they are and to whom they are not related by the ties of love; and knowing it for their own happiness, would be guided by this knowledge.

But what is this mystic power called love and from whence does it derive its potent power over mankind? In the first place genuine love is something beyond volition, and exists entirely indedendent of the will. There never was a love that was learned. A deep and sincere regard, even a pure affection, may be acquired; but love is the recognition of the relationship that exists naturally between the positive and negative conditions of matter. Wherever there are two or more elements blended, by attraction, there is the love of nature. Love, therefore, is the attraction of opposites by the inherent power of relation that exists, but can never be created. Hence in human beings, it is found exhibiting itself where it is least suspected to be possible. Moreover when the related elements exist in two persons, let them meet wherever they may it is impossible to avoid a mutual recognition, and let them be bound elsewhere in whatsoever manner, they must love, because they have no power to prevent it.

It is also to be observed that there are various degrees of love, all the way from the merest present exhibition, to the most complete blending. Hence there is need for freedom that the fittest may predominate, since if love at all be right, then the highest—the most perfect—should be the love that should control, and he or she who does not obey the higher love, sins against the law of love and must suffer the inexorable consequences of that law.

Therefore, from the point of present human happiness merely, the further we analyze this matter of love the more convincing the proofs become, that it must and will be free; and the more conclusive the evidence that, though the bodies of two may be kept asunder by the terrors of the law and a fearful crucifixion be thereby entailed upon them, yet their souls will mingle and the magic thrills of reciprocal feeling pass and repass whenever they come within the sphere of each other's influence. Is it not foolish then—aye, is it not more than this, is it not criminal, longer to attempt to place limits upon this heaven ordained passion? Shall we not the rather recognize the truth as stated by Pope when he says:

"Love free as air at sight of human ties,
Spreads his light wings and in a moment flies."

As the results of freedom for love, then, we may predicate the elevation of humanity out of the awful chasm of misery and despair into which it has been precipitated by slavery and the endeavor to escape or evade its duties, to purity, peace and happiness. We may expect from it that hypocrisy, deceit and lust will be banished the earth, and that in their places will be enthroned a love that shall seek to bless, instead of to possess, its object.

But a great many people say Oh, yes! I believe in free love, but not in free lust, meaning thereby that they believe in free love for such as are exactly upon their planes of love, but not for those who are not yet so far ascended. Now I am striving for freedom for all conditions; for those low down in the scale of development as well as for those higher up the ladder of progress. A freedom that grants less than this is despotism. If freedom be an inherent natural right, then all individuals of whatever status are entitled to it. The only limit that can be placed upon it is the boundary of its own sphere, so that the sphere of another shall not be invaded, without first obtaining the necessary consent. All sexual love based upon consent must be free love, since there is no compulsion involved.

What then are we to understand by free lust, and what do they mean who say they are in favor of the former but not of the latter? I have already defined love to be an attraction existing between opposites in sex, independent of the volition of either party, and sexual intercourse by such opposites as proper sexual conditions. It can make no difference whether those conditions continue an hour, a day or a lifetime. It is sufficient that they exist. But lust is the perverted action of the desire for sexual love exhibiting itself in masturbation, sodomy, purchased intercourse as in prostitution, or in enforced intercourse as in marriage; and to this sort of lust I am as much opposed as anybody can be—and therefore while the people will have marriage laws, I would also have laws to protect wives from the beastly lust that now prevails so fearfully in marriage, and by which thousands of wives are annually sent to untimely graves, and the world peopled by intellectual, moral, or social dwarfs and abortions.

Yes! it exists and what is the remedy? Why, simply the freedom that will permit this lust to exhibit itself in proper sexual relations and thus become love ; hence when freedom is inaugurated, lust will have lost its domain, and there will soon cease to be any such thing. But the objectors do not mean this, they mean that those who are inclined to constant change, shall not be permitted to change. But who is to decide when free .om is the rule? Surely not any individual for anybody but himself. So it matters not how promiscuously inclined anybody may be, there can be no possible right to restrain him, except through growth from his conditions. This whole matter must be remanded from the control of law to the sphere of education and growth. The person who desires promiscuous sexuality has just the same right to obtain it that he who desires pure monogamy has to obtain that. To state it differently: They who desire promiscuousness, have just as good a right to enforce it as a rule for society, as they who desire monogamy, have to enforce it as a rule. It is strange, however, how few people there are who are able to look at this question from a point of view opposite to their own.

Because I advocate the right of freedom for all classes, I am charged, as I said before, with advocating promiscuousness; but I can easily and clearly show the utter foolishness and the absurdity of that charge. I advocate the freedom for religion, to be enjoyed equally by the Christian, the Infidel, the Pagan and the Jew; but I am neither one or the other of any of these, but a Spiritualist. Now why is it not charged, because I advocate this freedom, that I advocate Paganism? Simply because I do not—and people are so well versed in religious affairs as not to make so ridiculous an assertion; but the same persons who would never think of charging me with the advocacy of fire-worship, because I advocate the right of the fire-worshiper, do not hesitate to charge me with promiscuousness because I advocate the right to that condition for those who desire it. Is there anybody here who fails to see the analogy or the inconsistency of my would be judges?

Since the manly letter of Moses Hull appeared in the WEEKLY, many persons have written to ask me if that is Woodhullism. I reply, No! That is Hullism without the Wood. But if there be anything that may with propriety, be called Woodhullism it is this right of everybody to their own lives. And for my part I wish that all professing spiritual teachers would be as honest as Moses and Elvira Hull have been, and tell us the results of their experiences. Should they do so, I have no doubt that many of them would excel their predecessors—the Hulls—in profitable lessons. I do not think I venture anything in saying if every person present, who has been before the people as a spiritual teacher, were to relate his or her sexual experiences truly, that from this day the revolution would be accomplished. Moses Hull writes in the last WEEKLY that more than fifty speakers have said to him privately: "I have lived the same life you have, and with the same results; but I am not a big enough fool to tell of it." A pretty lot of teachers, surely. They have lived a certain life from which they confess to having received benefit over the accepted methods, and yet they will not enlighten us by the facts of their experiences so that we may profit thereby.

Compared with such hypocrites, Moses Hull is an angel of light, and I trust the time will come, and that he will have no peace until it comes, when Moses Hull shall support his own statements by those of a similar character received from these persons who are afraid to be anything but hypocrites, so that the world may know how much of its happiness and goodly conditions depend upon such loves as it pretends to condemn; and more than this even: I hope and trust that he may be stung, if nothing else will do it, into reminding a few professing "immaculates" who have ministered to his relief, that it is not exactly in good taste to denounce those who advocate sexual freedom.

Mark me, as this warfare for our rights continues, every person who has lived a free life, which they now attempt to cover by the hue and cry of "Mad Dog" and "Stop Thief" will be compelled to stand unmasked before the world; and I can name a dozen, who now berate Moses Hull, who when this time shall come would gladly change places with him. This infernal hypocrisy and sham morality have got to be exposed and abolished. They are sapping the vitals of honor and truth, and threatening the existence of all faith in humanity.

Whatever you may say of "Woodhullism," it cannot be that it is rotten at the core, of deceit ; or that externally it is mildewed by hypocrisy. You may, however, if you will, slime it all over with freedom, sexual freedom if you please, for the highest as well as the lowest, for all grades and kinds, and I will still rejoice that this ism is affixed to my name. There is but one other word in which I glory more than in that of freedom, and that word is love—love, the fulfilling of the law. Love, all that we can know of God—indeed that is God. Oh! what possibilities cluster around that heavenly name, that shall be realized when, with it, is joined its needed counterpart, freedom—freedom for love—freedom in love—freedom to love ; and when it shall be the highest blessing of life to love and to be loved freely—when both men and women shall be able, with pride, to proclaim it to the world that they love, instead of as now, being compelled to shrink into the dark corners of the earth with their happiness, lest it be learned of men. Then indeed shall men and women be as the angels in heaven, who neither marry or are given in marriage, and heaven and earth be merged in one. Such is to be the fulfilling of the law, "that ye love one another."

But I must pass to another and still more momentous part of my subject. I have shown you why we die, and it is not because of our false religion, our politics or our lack of them; but because of our false sexual relations. Here is the cause, and here must we look for the remedy. But how obtain it ? I have told you that the inhabitants of the oldest planet, still die, and that as spirits, they are not yet resurrected; and also that the needed elements by which to arrive at this condition, must first be combined upon the earth, since here they are only to be found.

Now what does the resurrection, of which so much is said in all so-called holy, because inspired writings, mean ? Simply a return to physical life, as thousands of spirits have been endeavoring to do for the last few years; and only partly and unsatisfactorily, at best, succeeding. At most, admitting all that is claimed to be true, they are able merely to make themselves known to friends. Even this is a great success, and merits all the adoration that is given it; but what is this compared with that which shall be when this return shall be complete and made at will; when they shall return, and, assuming a body of flesh, abide again with us on the earth ? No spiritualist will be prepared to deny this possibility. Indeed I believe it is generally conceded, by spiritualists, that materialization will soon be perfected.

But do any consider what that means to us of earth ? Do any imagine that, when the great and good of spirit life, shall return and, in the flesh, abide with us, they will pay tribute or respect to the present order of social things? Will they, who thousands of years have been, as the angels in heaven, neither marrying nor given in marriage, conform to our laws which pretend to control sexual intercourse? will they marry their loves on earth legally ?

Perhaps some respectable Spiritualists who frown upon me for advocating an order of things that must be, before Materialization can be, had better set their faces against this new and dangerous thing, for I tell you that the spirits are coming back to tear your damned system of sexual slavery into tatters and consign its blackened remnants to the depth of everlasting hell. And would to Heaven they would come here to-night and confirm my words. You would believe them while you will not believe me, who now speak for them.

Do you not suppose that many, now on earth, are loved in heaven; and that when these spirits come again that that love will make itself manifest? Do you suppose they will care for your marriage laws? I tell you they will walk into your families and claim as their loves those who are held as slaves and carry them off before your very eyes. They will come to your daughters and inspire them with a love which, perhaps, they have never known. Will you turn your children from your doors, because, forsooth, they have dared to love a resurrected spirit, without having the consent of the Parson or the Squire? Bosh! I am disgusted with such pitiful morality, and I am sorry for those who have yet to be awakened to the fact that it is pitiful, who imagine that purity and virtue are lodged in a license which is granted by law, at a cost of twenty-five cents and upward, *permitting* people to consort sexually.

No! They will laugh at your professed ownership in sex, and tell you to enforce it if you can. They will snap their fingers at your officers and spit upon your laws as I have been taught by them, to do. Nor will they wait for divorces either. They will love whom they will; and in their loving, lift us of earth, to their level. I know there are thousands who have been sexually inspired of spirits; and many more whom spirits control and through whom they receive the benedictions of love. Once and for all I tell you, Oh, children of earth, that you had better put your houses in order and await the coming of the bridegroom or the bride. Accept sexual freedom while yet it can be attained, by degrees, and not wait until it shall tear your souls at its sudden coming. I know how hard it is to give up to the embrace of another the one whom you think you love, but whom you desire for selfish gratification rather than to bless. I know that it is often easier to yield life itself; and I have come to you, in time, to warn you to prepare for what is surely coming, aye, is even now at your very doors, liable to break in upon you and find you like the foolish virgins with your lamps untrimmed.

But the possibility of the resurrection of spirits involves another startling fact which has been, as yet, barely thought of. If the spirit world has so nearly approached this as to be on the point of being able to take on the body again at will, this world must be so near to the spirit world as to be able to throw off the body at will. Have you ever thought of this? Yet when you think of it you will see that it must be so. And this means the beginning of the final reunion of the inhabitants of the two worlds in a common brotherhood. Many of you already know that the spirit often leaves the body. You know that when many mediums are entranced, the resident spirit is absent from the body. What does all this mean, except it be the near approach to the possibility of leaving the body at will? It is the counterpart to the return of the spirits. Both spheres advance alike toward each other; and when the union shall come, it will not alone be spirits coming to earth but mortals going to heaven as well. Indeed, it will be both; and heaven and earth will then be forever merged in one.

Before this can be established everywhere, however, it must have a beginning somewhere; and from that, spread out to the broad universe. And it is to this point that all my remarks have tended. This is the question directly and first at issue. This solved, and all the rest shall come. I have already said that the Spirits, engaged in this movement, have concentrated all their power upon a single individual; and that all the opposition has also centered there; and the fiercest of battles has been waging for the last eighteen months. It was upon the point of being solved at that time, ago, but the ignorance, weakness and foolishness of the individual, thwarted it. The failure called the attention of the opponents to its near realization, and enabled them to renew the combat at that point; and thus it has waged; and thus it still wages, undecided. Meanwhile the time approaches, when it must be decided, or go by, and the world be remanded, as I said before, to a long age of darkness and desolation, compared to which there is nothing recorded in history. Civilization will be blotted out and the Spirit world shut from earthly view a million years. Is it any wonder that I am in earnest when I know these things are threatening? How can I hold my peace and see all this befall the fair earth and its civilization, which is so advanced on the road toward the millennial era; indeed is just about to enter upon it?

But what must this beginning be? Why, evidently the attainment of the power over death by a human being, to counterpart the power over life, by a Spirit; that is: an inhabitant of the earth-sphere, must attain to the condition of superiority over death, so as to counterpart the condition of an inhabitant of the Spirit-Sphere, with whom it is possible to assume, at will, the material form; that is, again, that a human being must attain a spiritualized materiality, such as Spirits will take on when they shall return. It will be readily understood that, when the final union has occurred; when Spirits become materialized, and human beings become Spiritualized, that the bodies in which both shall appear will be of the same etherialized material. Now this is what I mean, when I say there must be a beginning somewhere, in order that the desirable may spread everywhere. This beginning will be with a single individual, and when attained, there will be perfect Spirit Materialization. From this it will spread, through many, to all individuals both in and out of the present bodies.

The birth of the possibility; the first realization of the conditions, will be to the world like the birth of any new fact in science, to be rapidly made use of by persons here and there all over the world. Then when once the demonstration comes, it will run with lightning speed around the world and revolutionize every existing custom, form, law, and nearly every pretended science, and every habit of life.

Now, are you ready to receive what I was on the point of saying early in my subject? And will you accept it as coming from the Spirit world; from Spirits who represent the organized forces of that world, and who are to inaugurate their government on earth; coming from them through one who has had sufficient experience to know of her own knowledge that it is true?

I presume there may be a dozen persons, not more, in this hall who, at some time in their lives, have felt magnetic thrills, based on sexual contact, that for the time have transformed them, so that they scarcely knew whether they were in this or the other sphere, and which have lingered for months, in greater or less power; and many more who from, perhaps, the slightest touch of another, have felt the magnetic currents course every nerve in their bodies, but from the contact not proceeding to sexuality, not experiencing the perfect ecstasy of the other condition? Now, this condition is the perfect sexual blending of the sexes, and those between whom it exists are perfectly mated sexually, and married divinely. And it is, that every individual in the world may find his or her sexual mate who shall be this revelation, and arrive at this ethereal condition, that I have raised my voice, and suffered all I have for sexual freedom. And will any venture to say there is a single person in the whole world who is not insanely prejudiced against freedom, who does not desire to arrive at this condition; indeed who would not sell all that he has if, with the proceeds, it could be purchased?

This is what I mean by the impossibility of disease when perfect sexual conditions are present. Those who have any near approach to them cannot be sick; and those who shall have them perfected, cannot die. I say, some have experienced the conditions of which I speak; but not yet has anybody in the world gained them perfectly. The experiences that have occurred, and which are a prophecy of what is in store for every human being, have been impossible of continuation because of the preventing influences of our present system of social slavery. The subjects of them, preferring the approval of society, rather than the possession of eternal life (not contemplating that the condition meant the final triumph over death), have failed to be free, in which condition only it can come.

And what I mean by being free is, to be so far above caring for the world, or what it or anybody in it may say, as to stand boldly before it and live complete freedom. To be enslaved by public opinion, to be prevented from doing right from fear of what anybody may say or anybody do, is to be in a more cursed slavery than is that of law itself. I would rather be sold and delivered, by law, to a man, than to be compelled to live with him, not being married, from the force of public opinion. I tell you that many reformers are in a worse slavery than they are whom they would emancipate. And I know it.

There is a something abroad in the land, however, that assumes the name of freedom—in which to hide its deformities —against which I wish to declare my personal objections. It is that freedom which conceals itself behind the mask of hypoc risy; that seeks its own line of life while passing, for living something quite different   that has a make-believe love for the husband or the wife, while really loving elsewhere; that receives the caresses of the husband or wife, inwardly disgusted by them, while lavishing, those which proceed from the heart, elsewhere. Once, and for all time, permit me to say, that I hold this thing —which many people at present call freedom, and which many more live, and name it respectability—is the poison Upas tree of the present social condition, and the bane of freedom. Beside such damned hypocrisy as this, Moses and Elvira Hull are, in my esteem, as white as snow. People must live the lives with which they wish to stand accredited before the world. Then, and not till then, can there be freedom; since those who live a life they do not wish the world to know, are degraded slaves, as much below the negro or the legal slave, as he who wallows in bestiality for its own sake, is below her who sells her body to buy food for her starving children.

The new element that the Spirits require for the purposes of more effective and permanent materializations, is a spiritualized sexual aura, to be exhaled by the perfect blending of the sexes, in the highest and divinest relations known to humanity. The conditions, requisite to develop this element, reside, without question, in many individuals—many pairs of individuals; and without doubt, various temporary exhibitions of the perfect unity of these conditions have occurred, which, had there been unlimited freedom for their existence, might, ere this, have evolved what is required; hence, the triumph over slavery, in all its forms, must be, before these conditions can be, and continue. All things that operate as obstructions or hindrances, must be removed, so that the opposite poles of the battery may remain in undisturbed connection. Like the magnetic telegraph, the medium over or through which the positive and negative currents pass, must be unbroken and undisturbed. The foul atmosphere, arising from a diseased public opinion, must be corrected by the sanitary influence of some powerful disinfectant, so that its miasm may not blight the new-born life, nor poison its vigorous action. The child of heaven must live, even if all that is must die that it may live; but to no such extremity need things come, if the contaminating grasp of the despot be removed from the throat of freedom. and it be permitted to breathe, as if it had a right in the world. But there must be freedom before there can be life; and there must not be so much as a criticism, even, of public opinion, to prevent its full and free reception and action; nor to deter the people from seeking it with earnest desire.

I said in my Steinway Hall speech, "I am a Free Lover. I have an inalienable, constitutional and natural right to love whom I may; to love as long or as short a period as I can; to change this love every day if I please, and with this right neither you nor any law you can frame have any right to interfere." I will supplement this by saying now: That I will love whom I may; that I will love as long or as short a period as I can; that I will change this love whenever the conditions to which I have referred indicate that it ought to be changed; and that neither you nor any law you can make shall deter me. I hope everybody will understand just what sort of a Free Lover I am, and never have any more contention over it.

Now, do you not see the solution of this whole matter? The strife in life is to be, to attain to the condition of triumph over death, and this comes only by the perfect blending of two of opposite sex. To gain this there must be, as in every other department of discovery, freedom to experiment, until the law that governs it is discovered, when everybody will be able to know who is his negative or her positive.

I wish here, however, to explain what will be perhaps unwelcome to many, who think that promiscuousness is the process through which this boon is to be gained. I am sorry to feel compelled to disappoint their anticipations; but I do not mean, if I can help it, to be misunderstood about this matter any longer.

The law by which this attainment is governed is this: the greater the number of failures made by people in seeking their sexual mates, the greater the difficulty will be in mating when they are found. This will become evident when it is considered that every sexual act which is not the legitimate expression of sexual unity, has a deleterious effect on the sexual organs and impulse. This may be illustrated by the stomach. A hungry person may, in the absence of the most proper food, eat that which, not being best adapted to his condition, will produce derangement of the stomach; but which, nevertheless, serves to prevent starvation for the time. A sufficient continuance of this food will cause chronic dyspepsia, which will yield only when that which was needed at the outset to prevent the disease, is procured.

So also is it with Sexuality. Pure and perfect conditions and uses are as necessary to its health, as is proper food for the stomach. In the absence of perfect conditions, imperfect relations are maintained, which, continued indefinitely, produce chronic derangement — demoralization — of the organs, and through them, as I have shown, of the system generally, which derangements can be cured, only, by the perfect sexual blending of two perfectly or nearly related natures. Hence the young, who have never had sexual experience, are the foremost candidates for the new era of perpetuated life; while those who do not attain it, will continue to die and arrive at this condition from the opposite sphere by the opposite process, prolonged perhaps to hundreds of years.

Looking at this matter from another stand-point, it is seen that when its facts are recognized, as they will be, the whole social rule of society will be revolutionized, since the strife will then be for life, instead of for wealth; but I cannot enter upon this broad field now.

By this new motive, given to sexuality, it is, at once and forever, lifted from the mire and filth, into which it has been cast by the debaucheries of the world, consequent upon mistaken sexual restrictions, and seated upon the throne, it cometh to judge the world in righteousness. It is indeed the Christ that is to come, by whom every person shall be justified of himself and to himself; by whom alone can any man be saved from the vices, superstitions and miseries of earth-life. It is by this gate by which alone the kingdom of heaven—happiness—can be entered; and whether we first lay the mortal body in the ground, and enter it from the other sphere, having passed through the purgatory necessary to purge our sins; or been driven to the depths of the lowest hell by the tremendous weight of our iniquities, that they may be consumed by its quenchless fire; or whether we enter it by the direct and natural methods of regular growth—continuous evolution—without the descent into purgatory or hell, depends upon the use we shall make of this new-found salvation. This is not only to usher in the resurrection of the dead, and thus fulfill the Scripture, but also to unite the parts of the system of salvation, which are now scattered among the various religious beliefs, into one complete and perfect system for the whole world.

There has been personal experience sufficient to prove that what the spirits have told me about this matter, is true. Almost every woman, at some time in her life, has suffered from false sexual relations. Many who by nature are eminently endowed, sexually, seldom or never know delight, thinking the while that they love their husbands with their whole souls; but they will some time learn, that this is custom and education rather than genuine affection on the part of either. For years these endure sexual starvation, since starvation means unconsummated sexual desire. They lose their health, not knowing the cause. They grow old before they are fully matured in form, and some disease sets in that ultimately proves fatal, and of which it is imgined they die, while the real cause lies back in these false sexual relations.

But all these long weary years, there is a void in the inner soul of every woman, which tells spiritually and prophetically —for all women are endowed in this way to a greater or less extent—of a lover with whom she shall traverse the infinitude of futurity. In spirit dream she wanders the woods and hills with him, and gathers flowers of sweetest fragrance; and when some sorrow presses her heavily, his Spirit comforts and sooths. And when she meets, as meet all shall, oh what a revelation. Words are insignificant to express it. A new life dawns. A low and thrilling melody breaths transcendent strains of hope and fear, and the longing ear listens lest one sweet note escape, and the hope go by forever. The stars grow brighter; the moon fairer; the fields greener, and all nature roll onward in its mighty circuit, in an atmosphere of perfect joy. The heart beats faster; the eye sparkled with a new lustre; the crimson deepens on cheek and lip, the voice grows low and deep and tremulous; and the whole being thrills with ecstasy as it recognizes and embraces the companion so long watched and prayed for. The emaciated form assumes its rounded proportions; disease vanishes, and again she is a woman restored to her pristine beauty, vigor and life.

To sum up what I have to say on this most important of questions, and to generalize what I have said upon the subject of sexuality, I would repeat that the conditions under which progressive rejuvenation or immortality in the form may be attained, can only be secured under the auspices of absolute and entire freedom—a freedom not incompatible with perfect law, but its certain consequent and proper consummation. Let us hope that it may soon be established, notwithstanding the fact that it has taken ages to evolve the yet imperfect law which obtains among us. To the credit of our country, in our Revolutionary War we placed the keystone in the arch of man's spiritual freedom when we decreed in our Constitution, if not civil, at least religious liberty, and guaranteed it to our people by law. We must now advance upon that position and ordain Social Freedom, which is its natural ally, and its necessary aid and support.

And of all freedom that the spirit of man or woman can conceive, or the heart of woman or man can desire, the highest —Social Freedom—culminating in personal liberty, is the most valuable. It is the natural foundation, the true basis of all other liberties. We must affirm, and, as far as we are able, must secure for all human beings this most sacred of all rights —a right which belongs to every man and every woman (unconvicted of crime) at all times, in all places, and under all circumstances; and of all functions in the body of a man or woman to which this greatest of liberties most especially pertains, the sexual function is the most important: it must not and ought not to be disturbed in its offices by arbitrary laws, unless it unwarrantedly invades another's liberties; and the effort to reduce it to legal or religious bondage has resulted, and ever must result, in introducing into society misery, bestiality, anarchy and destruction. If we would change the present rotten state of the world with regard to our sexual horrors, all that we have to do is to acknowledge and inaugurate this grandest of all liberties; to recognize the right of woman to rule in the domain of the affections; to aid the full development of the natural love that yet exists between the sexes; and to guard our children from that ignorance in sexual matters which has decimated and is decimating the present generation of mankind.

Then, and not till then, when we have performed all the above-mentioned duties, may we look for our reward in that progressive and progressing life, which I believe is even now at our doors, waiting for admission. When that is obtained then shall we behold a light without a shadow, a morn without an eve, a day without a night. Then shall we be able to bridge over the gloomy chasm of death, and to build for ourselves a Jacob's ladder, reaching from earth to heaven, on which spirits and mortals will be perpetually engaged ascending and descending in unending harmony and felicity. It may be that not one of us may witness this fulfillment of the prophecies of the past; but, if we do our duty, we have every reason to hope, and I, for one, believe, that we shall soon succeed. We are now like Bunyan's Pilgrims in Doubting Castle the den of the giant Despair; but, like them also, we have a key in our bosoms that will unlock the gate of it, and let us out into the flower-spangled fields of pleasure and delight, and the name of that key is— Liberty!

Yes—Liberty! Full and free in all matters pertaining to humanity; civil, political, religious, social and sexual liberty. When that is attained, then may we hope by right education to achieve for men and women, that improvement and exaltation which we have already accomplished, by arbitrary laws, based upon those of nature, for flowers, fruits and animals. Then may we look to bid adieu to the miserable and deformed speci: mens of humanity, which now meet us on every side, too often exposing their infirmities as a means of soliciting our charity. Then may we aspire to see nations doing their duty by their children, extending their fostering care over them in their infancy, and bringing them up tenderly to labor and to love. Then may we expect woman to throw off the chains of the barbarisms of the fashions, and prove *in propria persona* that art cannot improve the charms which nature has lavished on her when following right counsels and obeying true laws. Then may we also find in man, not a pitiless tyrant absorbed in the pursuit of money, but a benign benefactor, the provider and careful distributor of the wealth of communities.

Oh! that these my earnest desires may speedily be realized! That the ghastly darkness in which the world is now involved with regard to sexual affairs may rapidly pass away! That, by the attainment of a better knowledge of ourselves we may be able to produce a very superior race of men and women to that at present existing! That the sexual miseries and bestialities of the present time may soon be annihilated forever! If I had the power I would unvail all the hidden horrors of the system which now are covered, to the scorn and loathing of the world; but I would do so, as the skillful surgeon dissects a rotten corpse, not to injure the dead—but to benefit the living:

I hack to teach; not mangle to expose.

But the world charges me with taking delight in so nauseous an occupation. It is mistaken. I would that my lot had fallen in pleasanter places; but it has not. Sufficient for me, and for all of us, if, in our passage through life. we perform our duties therein.

Alas! who should envy me my position? Fortune, fame,

a good name, even health itself, has been demanded from me in my work, and I have given—cheerfully given them all. I have been the sport of society—in many instances the rejected of the sex I have served and am serving so well. The debauched ruffian, tobacco-stained, and redolent with the fumes of whisky, points at me as something worse than himself. I have been for the past three years pitilessly lampooned and carricatured in lewd and impossible positions by execrable artists, in the public press; unjustly hounded out of my office by the minions of the law; my business destroyed without hope of renovation; torn from my family and illegally imprisoned for more than a month; excessive bail demanded from me, not for the purpose of security, but with intent to compass my further oppression; and all these for an act which has since been repeated by other journals, with additions—without punishment. Added to this, as a consequent of the intense mental anxiety arising from judgment deferred, I have been stricken almost to death, having been in a comatose state for many hours, so that my life was, for a long time, almost despaired of by my nearest friends and kindred. Yet—in spite of all this—I am here, unchanged, fighting the old, old battle for the liberty of woman, and the consequent exaltation of man.

Neither do I despair of the cause I advocate, or mourn over the price it has cost me. Individual personal freedom, culminating in perfect sexual liberty, is indeed a pearl of great price, whose value is beyond computation. It cannot be too dearly purchased, for in it is hidden the world's regeneration; and, whatever may be said of those who battle for it, the future is certain to do justice to their memories, and crown them with garlands of honor. Nor will their recompense be alone the applause of humanity in after times, but they will receive a more immediate reward for their exertions in the cause of virtue and of justice, in that glorious Summer Land, to which we are all rapidly hastening—that happy place, where peace and delight are the prizes awarded to all who have developed their own souls here, by performing their duties freely toward their fellow-mortals.

And although, at the present time, in the industrial, civil, financial, intellectual and social world, every thing appears to be in chaotic confusion, I have the faith to believe, that the picture of the future I previously painted will soon be succeeded by a glorious and unending reality. Is it wicked for me to wish for the realization of such a vision? That human beings may speedily be relieved from their fetters, and men and women walk forth free in the light of perfect purity, holiness, liberty and love. Surely not! In the language of the ancient seer, then, let m conclude this lecture, calling upon all of you to aid in bringing forward so blessed a consummation. "And the Spirit and the Bride say—Come —and let him that heareth, say—Come!—and let him that is athirst—Come! And whosoever will, let him drink of the 'Water of Life' freely.

CHAPTER 5

Tried as by Fire; or,
The True and The False Socially
An Oration

Introduced by Michael W. Perry

With her 1874 "Tried as by Fire," Victoria Woodhull spoke again to a general audience rather than to fellow Spiritualists. According to her, this speech was given on "one hundred and fifty consecutive nights" to an audience of "a quarter of a million people." Since that was before radio and television, and her remarks were often reported by newspapers, in the 1870s she was one of the most widely heard women in America.

Assuming those speeches were as long as this roughly 22,000-word pamphlet, delivering each meant at least two hours of speaking without the benefit of a public address system to an often skeptical crowd averaging 1600 people.[1] It must have been exhausting work and was certainly financially necessary. As Mary Gabriel points out, on Friday, September 18, 1873 "thirty New York City banks and brokerage firms collapsed and the stock market was temporarily suspended. By January, five thousand businesses had been forced to close in what would be the nation's worst economic crisis to date."[2]

Woodhull's finances, already shaky, were worsened by the stock market crash. So she took to the road doing what she did best— speaking on controversial topics. In front of respectable audiences, she called for an end to marriage (page 5 in her text), accused husbands of being rapists (8), and condemned priests, lawyers, the press, and all who dared to disagree with her (4, 14). Women were not spared her fury. She claimed "that nine women in ten are so diseased, sexually, as to make them unfit to become mothers." (33) She promoted eugenics, then called stirpiculture, as the answer to virtually all social ills. Her social schemes went beyond ending marriage. Anticipating what the feminist sociologist Charlotte Perkins Gilman would later advocate, she called

1. Lois Beachy Underhill lists some of the cities Woodhull visited in *The Woman Who Ran for President*, 160. Others are mentioned in the 300 pages of "Press Notices" in Woodhull's *The Human Body the Temple of God* (1890).
2. Mary Gabriel, *Notorious Victoria: The Life of Victoria Woodhull* (Chapel Hill: Alonquin Books, 1998), 119.

for "isolated households" to be replaced by "co-operative homes" and "immense hotels" run by a "grand industrial organization" (44) that would rule the world. Those who came to be titillated got their money's worth, although some newspaper reporters complained that she wasn't as radical as they expected. Perhaps they weren't listening.

"Tried as by Fire" is her most revealing free love speech, exposing a broad social agenda in which eugenics was becoming more important than free love. In it she made clear why she had declared war on marriage: "First, because it stands directly in the way of any improvement in the race, insisting upon conditions under which improvement is impossible; and second, because it is, as I verily believe, the most terrible curse from which humanity now suffers, entailing more misery, sickness, and premature death than all other causes combined." (7)

She took up the second reason first. Prominent among the causes of ill-health, she said, was marital rape: "Night after night there are thousands of rapes committed, under cover of this accursed license; and millions—yes I say it boldly, knowing whereof I speak—millions of poor, heart-broken, suffering wives are compelled to minister to the lechery of insatiable husbands, when every instinct of body and sentiment of soul revolts in loathing and disgust." (8)

It's easy to suspect rhetorical exaggeration. Just after those remarks, she drew an analogy with slavery: "Is this too sweeping? What was it that condemned slavery? Was it that all slaves were cruelly treated? Not the most ultra-Abolitionist ever pretended it! They admitted that the majority were contented, comfortable, and happy. Can the same be said, truly, of the slaves to marriage, now?" (9) All too briefly, Woodhull let slip that most women were happy with their marriages. It was her ideology that it was "the most consummate outrage on women," (3) that drove her forward, finding fault after fault.

When it was useful rhetorically to admit that most men were not depraved beasts, she shifted easily to a contrary point of view. For those who ask how children would be cared for, she argued that even without legal compulsion, men are devoted fathers who would not "abandon their children if the law of marriage were repealed." (11) But if no law is required to make them kind to their children, why was radical legal change necessary to make them kind to the women in their lives?

To some extent, Woodhull's ideology reflected her own bitter first experience of marriage. Almost twenty pages later she used her mentally retarded son, Bryon, to illustrate the result of marital rape.

> My boy, now nineteen years of age, who should have been my pride and my joy, has never been blessed by the dawning of reasoning. I was married at fourteen, ignorant of every thing that related to my maternal functions. For this ignorance, and because I knew no better than to surrender my maternal functions to a drunken man, I am cursed with this living death.... Do you think that I can ever cease to hurl the bitterest imprecations against the accursed thing that has made my life one long misery? Do you think that I can ever hesitate to warn the young maidens against my fate, or to advise them never to surrender the control of their maternal functions to any man!" (27)

Two pages later, she returned to her first and more important reason for eliminating marriage. "There can be a better race," she said, "only by having better children." (29) She then explained how to get better children. At that time and like many others, Woodhull believed that children were heavily influenced by the experiences a mother has during pregnancy. She gave as an example a woman who brought her son to a Wisconsin speech. While that woman "was carrying him she was in the habit of going into her uncle's liquor store and tasting his liquor." (30) The result was that the son's chest was marked with bottles, and "the young man is a confirmed drunkard." Woodhull went on to claim that, "The power of the mother over the unborn child, for evil, is too well-attested by too many facts to need further elucidation." (30)

Ten pages later, she explained how a mother could be a force for good. Those who have read "The Elixir of Life" (Chapter 4), know that, when she told this general audience that she came upon the idea "clairvoyantly," she meant messages from spirits on other worlds.

> I have been shown, instinctively, as you would call it, clairvoyantly as I would say, the solution of this whole matter; but have not yet been able to reason it out so as to demonstrate it logically. But when impregnation takes place under perfect conditions of love and desire and their mutual consummation, the same process occurs regarding physical impurities as related to the new germ life, that takes place when water is changed to ice. For instance, ice formed from salt water is not salt ice. Salt is a foreign substance to water, and in its natural

changes is cast off. So impurities of the human system are foreign substances, which in perfected sexual conditions, form no part of the transmitted qualities. (38)

In those few words, we have why Woodhull thought eliminating marriage would create a superior race. Marriage meant sex often came at times other than "under perfect conditions of love and desire," and thus without the mystical 'ice from salt water' purifying process that produced superior children.

Science would never find evidence for what even Woodhull could not argue logically. Her own hostility to marriage would mellow with her third marriage. But her commitment to eugenics remained strong and adapted to more scientific beliefs. That change is reflected in how she explained her retarded son in this 1874 pamphlet, compared with what she wrote in her 1893 pamphlet, "The Scientific Propagation of the Human Race." There she explained Bryon's deficiencies this way:

The marriages of the immature also curse humanity by producing individuals who exhibit every stage of mental defect, from absolute idiocy to those who are simply stupid. The case may be cited of a girl who was left in ignorance of the simplest laws regarding her being. She was a victim of this ignorance; she became a mother at fourteen. Her child is an imbecile. The father and mother of the girl love this grandchild and deplore the fact that it is an imbecile. They are too ignorant to realise what caused this human failure. Marriage among the wealthier and better educated of the community is tending to be deferred. Among the poorer and most destitute the age of marriage has a tendency to become earlier. From these immature marriages offspring will be born who again will do little to raise the standard of humanity, who will not be deterred from procreating their kind from any consideration of right. Children born during the period of maximum vigour of the parents have, as a rule, the greatest physical and mental vigour. What must be the result then in children born of devitalized parents? In the marriages of those individuals who have no natural affinity for each other, where other inducements than love determine their union, the offspring exhibit analogous physical defects. The case is the same in the offspring of parents who are too similar in defects of constitution.[3]

---

3. Victoria Woodhull, *Lady Eugenist* (Seattle: Inkling Books, 2005), 282–83. From pages 14–15 in the original "The Scientific Propagation of the Human Race."

A vague lack of "natural affinity" had become just one cause among many for the birth of inferior children. Marriage was no longer the root problem, nor was free love the solution. Her eugenics had changed from mystical views about sex inspired by spirits to beliefs based on science and obsessed with the difference in birthrates between "the wealthier and better educated" and "the poorer and most destitute." Some of her later ideas were present in embryonic form in 1874. She anticipated those who, like the Swedish feminist Ellen Key, would make a new religion of eugenics, when she wrote the following:

> If either or both of the parties to a union have generally poor physical health—suffer from any chronic disease—such parties have unnatural and unhelpful sexual relations, and their progeny will be puling [crying, whining, whimpering], weakly, miserable, damned. Such a union is God-condemned if it have the approval of all the laws, and the blessing of all the priests in the world. (15)

Woodhull also anticipated a controversy that would trouble 'old stock' New Englanders during the late nineteenth and early twentieth century. She did so in these 1874 remarks:

> I do not complain of women as willfully sending the race onward to destruction. I only wish to show them that they are doing it, and to urge them by every argument that my woman's nature can suggest, or my mother's heart conceive, to stop the desolation. What can I say?... Shall I tell them that the birth-rate among the more intelligent classes has decreased one-half in twenty years by abortions; and that, unless these things cease, the race will ultimately be blotted out! (32)

What Woodhull was suggesting came to be called positive eugenics, a belief that the "more intelligent classes" should raise their birthrates, in this case by voluntarily having fewer abortions. Judging by her later speeches, Woodhull did not pursue that path, and in the next paragraph she turned to a more appealing topic for her, negative eugenics.

> Or shall I turn to the other side of the picture and show them the awful fact that nine women in ten are so diseased, sexually, as to make them unfit to become mothers, brought to this condition by their efforts to prevent pregnancy, or to procure abortions, or by continually submitting to undesired intercourse until the sexual instinct is dead; and that if these conditions go on for twenty years it will be impossible for women even to become pregnant. (33)

Woodhull's remark has two parts. The first was observational, "the awful fact that nine women in ten are so diseased, sexually, as to make them unfit to become mothers." That's the same figure she used in "The Scare-crows of Sexual Slavery" (Chapter 3), so it's not a passing fancy. In the second, she offered the behavioral and environmental cause. The efforts these women made to avoid children—caustic birth control chemicals and primitive abortions, along with what two paragraphs later she called being "constantly debauched by the insatiable lusts of their husbands," had made them "unfit to become mothers." That's why on the next page she wanted a "solemn conclave" at which women swear to "never again become pregnant of an undesired child." Her mysticism led her to believe that desiring sex and a child would banish disease (see Chapter 4, particularly page 102).

We should not forget that at this time Woodhull wasn't focused on heredity. Few people were. She had looked around and concluded that ten percent of the population were 'fit' to have children, but were having too few. The other ninety percent were "unfit" parents for various reasons and having too many. What was to be done depended on the cause.

She then made a remark that, if true, suggests the history of eugenics may need substantial revision. Judging by the "scientific journals and monthlies," she said, her role as a controversial speaker had "awakened investigation on this subject. If all I have said is in error; if the truth lie in altogether different directions from those in which I point, out of the discussion now going on the truth will be evolved." (34) She believed she was the first to call attention to the problem, but thought others might better explain the cause and cure.

The next paragraph hints that this "evolved" truth might take a heredity bent. She quotes an April 6 (probably 1874) editorial in the Chicago *Times*, the "most influential and widely circulated journal of the great North-West." It suggests not only heredity as the cause, but raises the spectre of coercion to achieve a scientific "millennium."

... "Could society by some omnipotent fiat determine that, from to-day no sexual intercourse should occur, save in cases where there is a *mens sana in corpore sana* (meaning sound minds in sound bodies) less than half a century hence would witness the closing of hospitals, saloons, penitentiaries and 'houses;' the extinction, almost to a man, of physicians; and the cessation of nearly every movement whose purpose is the lessening of human suffering and vice. Taxes would sink to the minimum; men and women would tread the earth with the springy, buoyant step of perfect health; and the millennium would commence its glorious reign upon this our sin-bestridden and disease-cursed earth." (34–35)

The idea that controlled breeding would eliminate hospitals, saloons and prisons was ridiculous. Even with perfect heredity, hospitals would be needed for accidents, epidemics, and old age. Saloons exist wherever people are bored and lonely, and raising the average intelligence would only make criminals smarter. That 1874 editorial illustrates how many in the press often place an undue faith in what science can do and (rightly) suggests they would eagerly support eugenic sterilization (1920s) and eugenic abortion (1960s).

In two years the scientific trend Woodhull had noted and that she believed she created would have a momentous event. In 1876, newspapers reported that Richard L. Dugdale (1841–1883) had discovered a family in New York that he gave the name of "Jukes." The title of a book he published the next year summarized his claims: *The Jukes: A Study in Crime, Pauperism, Disease and Heredity*. He had begun his research in 1874, the very year Woodhull was making this speech in what the title page calls "the principle cities and towns of the country." Woodhull even mentioned Dugdale's research in an 1876 Boston speech.[4]

Today, that research is ridiculed, but we should not forget that for half a century (until the late 1920s), it was well-respected and opposed mostly by religious conservatives. In 1912, Henry Goddard would report similar results in *The Kallikak: A Study in the Heredity of Feeblemindeness*, and in 1916, Arthur H. Estabrook would update Dugdale's research with *The Jukes in 1915*. In her 1922 *The Pivot of Civilization*, the birth control pioneer Margaret Sanger (1879–1966) claimed: "Eugenics is chiefly valuable in its negative aspects. It is 'negative eugenics' that has studied the histories of such families as the Jukeses and the Kallikaks,

---

4. Victoria Woodhull, *Lady Feminist*, (Seattle: Inkling Books, 2005), 52. From the *Boston Herald*, Oct. 2, 1876. Woodhull was living in New York City and her speeches between 1871–74 could have influenced Dugdale's research in New York prisons that began in 1874. In turn, he may have influenced her later views on the causes and cures of social ills. Dugdale, an English 'gentleman scientist,' may have also been influenced by Francis Galton (1822–1911), a fellow English scientist, and Cesare Lombroso (1835–1909), an Italian criminologist.

that has pointed out the network of imbecility and feeblemindedness that has been sedulously spread through all strata of society."[5]

As Woodhull hinted in this speech, her eugenic arguments "evolved" (34) over time. Becoming less mystical and more scientific, they followed the path laid down by a Juke-justified emphasis the heredity of socially troublesome groups. Her pioneering role in developing what would become the dominant feminist point of view is why this book's companion volume, *Lady Eugenist*, has the subtitle, *Feminist Eugenics in the Speeches and Writings of Victoria Woodhull.*

Progressive-minded and scientific, mainstream feminism could not challenge the core belief of eugenics—a Darwinian division of races into superior and inferior with progress dependent on the relative birthrates of the two. Rebelling against the traditional woman's role as wife and mother, it also could not accept the lifestyle restrictions demanded by positive eugenics. To even suggest that was to call for 'forced motherhood' and what Margaret Sanger would attack as an unacceptable "cradle competition" between the fit and unfit.[6]

That left only negative eugenics. Science, ideology, and self-interest drove feminists such as Margaret Sanger and Britain's Marie Stopes (1880–1958) to follow in Woodhull's footsteps and support harsh measures to deal with what they regarded as a growing problem with "imbecility and feeblemindedness." In her 1938 autobiography, Sanger would hint at Woodhull's free love advocacy when she said, "Eugenics, which had started long before my time, had once been defined as including free love and prevention of conception."[7]

We should not forget, however, that all this began when Woodhull grasped at a strange and mystical form of eugenics to justify her own sexual lifestyle. Only later did her interest in eugenics grow in importance and evolve into a science-based ideology that stood on its own and became what she may have regarded as the most important cause in her long and active life. For more on that part of her life, you will need to read *Lady Eugenist*.

---

5. Michael W. Perry, ed. *The Pivot of Civilization in Historical Perspective* (Seattle: Inkling Books, 2003), 236. See also p. 79f.

6. *The Pivot of Civilization in Historical Perspective*, 90, 187, 233.

7. *The Pivot of Civilization in Historical Perspective*, 27.

TRIED AS BY FIRE;

OR,

THE TRUE AND THE FALSE,

SOCIALLY.

AN ORATION DELIVERED BY

VICTORIA C. WOODHULL,

IN ALL

The Principal Cities and Towns of the Country during an
engagement of

ONE HUNDRED AND FIFTY CONSECUTIVE NIGHTS,

TO AUDIENCES TOGETHER NUMBERING,

A QUARTER OF A MILLION OF PEOPLE.

. ·•· .

New York:
WOODHULL & CLAFLIN.
1874.

TRIED AS BY FIRE;

OR, THE TRUE AND THE FALSE, SOCIALLY.

For what purpose has this audience assembled; and what does it expect of me? Consider this question well now, since I propose to perform my duty regardless alike of approval or disapproval. In this duty you may listen to speech, such as, perhaps, you never heard from a public platform before.

You have been invited to hear the social problem discussed; to see it placed in the crucible of analysis to be tried by the hot, flames of truth, the fire meanwhile fed by stern facts, and stirred to intensest heat, until the dross shall rise to the surface and gradually disappear in fumes which may be unpleasant to the senses, but leaving behind the purified residuum gathered, indicating clearly what is true and what false in the tested subject —the sexual relations.

This is my task, not to be explained as it progresses in terms of glittering generalities, or of poetic fancy, or in gingerly words that may leave any in doubt as to what is intended, but plainly, honestly and earnestly, so that no one can misunderstand; but which will clearly set forth the conditions requisite to the health of these relations and the ignorance and abuse producing their diseases, and show what all knew, well enough, but few dare acknowledge to themselves, even: that there is much that is rotten in Denmark.

You are here as my guests, knowing in advance upon what subject I should speak; and I shall expect from you, individually and collectively, that courteous treatment which would be my due under any other circumstances than these, in which I might be your hostess, and you my guests. I shall not utter a word, phrase or sentence, except such as I conscientiously believe to be true, and that ought, for the good of the race, to be uttered. Nor shall I, in the course of my speech, plain, bold, even bald as it may be, use any expressions that, by the remotest construction, trench upon the boundaries of the vulgar. I shall, however, call things by their plain, Saxon names, holding that there is no part of the beautiful, human mechanism for which the pure in heart and thought ought be able to blush while it is under consideration.

I have asked this question and given this explanation for the purpose, at the outset, of permitting any here, who may not desire to listen to such plain speech as I have indicated, to retire now, so that others may not be disturbed, later in the evening, by their removal.

We now understand each other. It is not expected, it is not desired, that I withhold any fact I may have to offer, or advice I may have to give, regarding a subject which, more than any other, ought to command the attention of all enlightened people; but which, from falsely conceived ideas and a wrongly educated public opinion, is, more than any other, anathematized by almost the whole world.

People may pretend to blush, and the editors may write of me as indecent and vulgar, and say I have no shame to speak as I shall, what they will not dare to print. But, after all, ought not they and you and I rather to blush with real shame that such things as I shall mention, exist to be spoken about? I say, shame upon the newspapers, upon the preachers, teachers and doctors, that it is necessary for me to tell you what they ought long ago to have freely discussed, and have thus relieved me of this unpleasant task! I say, shame upon them all! and if the papers must perforce reproduce this word, let them be honest enough to properly apply it to the existing facts that of themselves are obscene and vulgar, and not to the speaker, who deals with them, not because it is either her nature or pleasure, but because she desires, like Boards of Health dealing with nuisances, to abate them.

Therefore if any vulgar or indecent thoughts arise in the mind of any person when these things are discussed, they do not attach to the speaker, but belong wholly to the individual; hence whatever may be thought now, or said hereafter, by any of you, or written about them at any time, is, by no possible, farfetched construction, an insult or imputation offered me. On the contrary it is a degradation to their subjects or authors, indicating the moral standpoint from which they, and not I, view the subject; and an insult to their mothers, to be explained by bad rearing and worse moral teaching. So do not think that, when I pick up the paper and read the nasty things that are said of me, I feel insulted or hurt; but rather believe that I pity those who write them, and feel that they have need of a loving mother or a darling sister, to snatch them from a degradation in which they can see only vulgarity or vileness, where there is really, nothing except purity and holiness.

If any of these mothers or sisters have such sons or brothers, let me beg of them to never let their yearning affections cease their efforts, nor their entreaties and tears to flow, until they are rescued—until they are restored to manhood.

No man who respects his mother or loves his sister, can speak disparagingly of any woman; however low she may seem to have sunk, she is still a woman. I want every man to remember this. Every woman is, or, at some time, has been a sister or daughter; and if she be now "out upon the cold world," do not forget that some son or brother helped, perhaps forced her there. Nor can it be amiss for men to ask: "Am I pure enough to make my judgments just?"

Let these thoughts check the rising frown and the cruel words you would bestow upon any unfortunate woman, in whatever condition, and call forth your love and sympathy instead, in some practical way for her rescue or assistance.

[Thus preliminarily introduced, I pass to the consideration of the true and the false in the relation of the sexes:]

The sexual relations of humanity are fundamental to its continuous existence, and are, therefore, the most important into which men and women enter. It is vital that they should be entered into properly, that they should be understood clearly, and, still more so, that they should be lived rightly. Nevertheless, the world has virtually declared that this shall not be. It denies all knowledge of them to the young, and permits the youth and the maiden to walk blindfolded into their exploration, ignorant even of their own functions, only taking special care that the journey, once begun, may never be retraced or stopped. It has left the travelers, as it were, in the mid-ocean of what may be their eternal happiness, if the course pursued be right; or their certain destruction if the chosen way be wrong, without chart or compass, subjected to winds which drive them, they know not where, and to currents and counter-currents, for which no haven of safety is provided; and, alas! they too often go down to untimely graves, victims to a willful ignorance. Such are the results of modern social regulations.

I am conducting a campaign against marriage, with the view of revolutionizing the present theory and practice. I have strong convictions that, as a bond or promise to love another until death, it is a fraud upon human happiness; and that it has outlived its day of usefulness. These convictions make me earnest, and I enter the fight, meaning to do the institution all possible harm in the shortest space of time; meaning to use whatever weapons may fall in my way with which to stab it to the heart, so that its decaying carcase may be buried, and clear the way for a higher and a better institution.

I speak only what I know, when I say that the most intelligent and really virtuous people of all classes have outgrown this institution; that they are constantly and systematically unfaithful to it; despise and revolt against it as a slavery; and only submit to a semblance of fidelity to it, from the dread of a falsely educated public opinion and a sham morality, which are based on the ideas of the past, but which no longer really represent the convictions of anybody.

Nor is this hypocritical allegiance the only or the greatest or gravest consideration that is capturing the opinions of the really intelligent. It is rapidly entering into the public thought, that there should be, at least, as much attention given to breeding and rearing children, as is given to horses, cattle, pigs, fowls and fruit. A little reflection shows that the scientific propagation of children is a thing of paramount importance; as much above and beyond that of personal property as children are above dogs and cats. And this conviction, practically considered, also shows that the union of the sexes, for propagation, should be consummated under the highest and best knowledge, and in such manner and by such methods as will produce the best results. These considerations are so palpable that they cannot be ignored; and they look to the early supercedure of the institution of marriage by some better system for the maintenance of women as mothers, and children as progeny. This is as much a foregone conclusion with all the best thinkers of to day as was the approaching dissolution of slavery, no more than ten years before its final fall.

But in the meantime men and women tremble on the verge of the revolution, and hesitate to avow their convictions; but aware of their rights, and urged by the impulses of their natures, they act upon the new theories while professing allegiance to the old. In this way an organized hypocrisy has become a main feature of modern society, and poltroonery, cowardice and deception rule supreme in its domain. The continuation of such falsity for a generation, touching one of the most sacred interests of humanity, will eradicate the source of honesty from the human soul. Every consideration of expediency, therefore, demands that some one lead the van in a relentless warfare against marriage, so that its days may be made short.

This is my mission. I entered the contest, bringing forward, in addition to the wise and powerful words of others, such arguments as my own inspirations and reflections suggested. No sooner had I done this, however, than the howl of persecution sounded in my ears. Instead of replying to my arguments, I was assaulted with shameful abuse; and I was astonished to find that the most persistent and slanderous and foul-mouthed accusations came from precisely those whom I happened often to know should have been, from their practices, the last to raise their voices against any one, and whom, if I had felt so disposed, I could have easily silenced. But simply as personality or personal defense, or spiteful retort, I have almost wholly abstained during these years of sharp conflict from making use of the rich resources at my command for this kind of attack and defense, and, passing the vile abuse which has beset me, have steadfastly pressed on in the warfare.

In a single instance only have I departed from this course. Circumstances conspired to put me in possession of certain facts regarding the most prominent divine in the land, and from him I learned that he too was not only false to the old dispensation, but unfaithful to the new—a double hypocrisy, over which I hesitated many months, doubting if I should use it. It was not that I desired or had any right to personally attack this individual; but something had to be done to break down the partition walls of prejudice that prevented public consideration of the sexual problem, and fully to launch it upon the tide of popular discussion. This revolution, like every other that ever preceded it, and as every other that ever will follow it, must have its terrific cost, if not in blood and treasure, then still in the less tangible but equally real sentimental injury of thousands of sufferers. It was necessary that somebody should be hurt. I cast the thunderbolt into the very centre of the socio-religio-moralistic camp of the enemy and struck their chieftain, and the world trembled at the blow. In twenty years not anybody will say that I was wrong, any more than anybody now says that the old leaders of the anti-slavery revolution were wrong in attacking slavery in the concrete.

My purpose was accomplished. Whereas, before, none had dared to broach the sexual question, it is now on everybody's lips; and where it would have been impossible for a man, even, to address a public, promiscuous audience anywhere without being mobbed, a woman may now travel the country over, and from its best rostrums, speak the last truth about sexuality, and receive respectful attention, even enthusiastic encouragement. The world has come to its senses—has been roused to the real import and meaning of this terrible question, and to realize that only through its full and candid examination may we hope to save the future from utter demoralization.

But why do I war upon marriage? I reply frankly: First, because it stands directly in the way of any improvement in the race, insisting upon conditions under which improvement is impossible; and second, because it is, as I verily believe, the most terrible curse from which humanity now suffers, entailing more misery, sickness and premature death than all other causes combined. It is at once the bane of happiness to the present, and the demon of prophetic miseries to the future—miseries now concealed beneath its deceptive exterior, gilded over by priestcraft and law, to be inwrought in the constitutions of coming generations to mildew and poison their lives.

Of what in reality does this thing consist, which, while hanging like a pall over the world, is pretendedly the basis of its civilization? The union of the opposites in sex is an instinct inherent in the constitutions of mankind; but legal marriage is an invention of man, and so far as it performs anything, it defeats and perverts this natural instinct. Marriage is a license for sexual commerce to be carried on without regard to the consent or dissent of this instinct. Everything else that men and women may desire to do, except to have sexual commerce, may be and is done without marriage.

Marriage, then, is a license merely—a permission to do something that it is inferred or understood ought not to be done without it. In other words, marriage is an assumption by the community that it can regulate the sexual instincts of individuals better than they can themselves; and they have been so well regulated that there is scarcely such a thing known as a natural sexual instinct in the race; indeed, the regulations have been so at war with nature that this instinct has become a morbid disease, running rampant or riotous in one sex, and feeding its insatiable maw upon the vitality of the other, finally resulting in disgust or impotency in both.

Isn't this a pretty commentary on regulation? Talk of Social Evil bills! The marriage law is the most damnable Social Evil bill—the most consummate outrage on woman—that was ever conceived. Those who are called prostitutes, whom these bills assume to regulate, are free women, sexually, when compared to the slavery of the poor wife. They are at liberty, at least to refuse; but she knows no such escape. "Wives, submit yourselves to your husbands," is the spirit and the universal practice of marriage.

Of all the horrid brutalities of this age, I know of none so horrid as those that are sanctioned and defended by marriage. Night after night there are thousands of rapes committed, under cover of this accursed license; and millions—yes, I say it boldly, knowing whereof I speak—millions of poor, heart-broken, suffering wives are compelled to minister to the lechery of insatiable husbands, when every instinct of body and sentiment of soul revolts in loathing and disgust. All married persons know this is truth, although they may feign to shut their eyes and ears to the horrid thing, and pretend to believe it is not. The world has got to be startled from this pretense into realizing that there is nothing else now existing among pretendedly enlightened nations, except marriage, that invests men with the right to debauch women, sexually, against their wills. Yet marriage is held to be synonomous with morality! I say, eternal damnation sink such morality!

When I think of the indignities which women suffer in marriage, I cannot conceive how they are restrained from open rebellion. Compelled to submit their bodies to disgusting pollution! Oh, Shame! where hast thou fled, that the fair face of womanhood is not suffused with thy protesting blushes, stinging her, at least into self-respect, if not into freedom itself! Am I too severe? No, I am only just!

Prate of the abolition of slavery! There was never servitude in the world like this one of marriage. It not only holds the body to whatever polluting use—abstracting its vitality, prostituting its most sacred functions, and leaving them degraded, debauched and diseased—but utterly damning the soul for all aspiration, and sinking it in moral and spiritual torpor. Marriage not slavery! Who shall dare affirm it? let woman practically assert her sexual freedom and see to what it will lead! It is useless to mince terms. We want the truth; and that which I have about this abomination I will continue to give, until it is abolished.

It is useless to cry, "Peace! Peace! when there is no peace." It is worse than useless to cry, Freedom! Freedom! when there is nothing but slavery. Let those who will, however, in spite of the truth, go home and attempt to maintain it there, and they will wake up to find themselves sold, delivered and bound, legally, to serve their masters sexually, but, refusing to do which, there will be a penalty, if not the lash. Now, husbands! now, wives! isn't this true? You know it is. And isn't it shameful that it is true?

Is this too sweeping? What was it that condemned slavery? Was it that all slaves were cruelly treated? Not the most ultra-Abolitionist ever pretended it! They admitted that the majority were contented, comfortable and happy. Can the same be said, truly, of the slaves to marriage, now?

But it was claimed and proven, as I claim and shall prove of marriage, that the instances of extreme cruelty were sufficiently numerous to condemn the system, and to demand its abolition. Proportionally, the instances of extreme cruelty in marriage are double what they were in slavery, and cover a much broader field, involving all the known methods by which the body can be tortured and the heart crushed. I could narrate personal cases of various kinds, for a week, and not exhaust my stock; but I cannot pause to do so. Judged by the logic of the past, this institution stands condemned, and will be soon relegated to the limbo of the past.

But there is another picture of this holy institution, scarcely less to be deprecated than are its actual cruelties; and little, if any, less degrading to womanhood: All men and women now living together, who ought to continue to so live, would so continue were marriage laws repealed. Is this true or false? This depends upon the truth or falsity of the following further propositions: Marriage may be consummated by men and women who love mutually; or, marriage may be consummated by men and women who have no love. If it be said that the former is false and the latter true, it is denied that love has anything to do with marriage—an affirmation, virtually, that they who hate may marry rightly; but if, on the contrary, the former is true and the latter false, it is agreed, constructively, that all I ever said or ever can say is true,

Now which is it? Has love, or ought it to have anything to do with marriage? Who will dare say that love should not be a precedent to marriage? But when this is affirmed, the legitimate corollary is not seen: That, since marriage should not begin without love, it should cease when love is gone. To accept the former, is to declare the latter. And no logician, however subtle, can escape it. Nor can you escape it; nor could I, although I labored for years to do so.

But if there are any who are in doubt as to what is right and true, I offer a test that will decide it. Let the married who live together, who would separate were the law repealed, rise!

Not any here of that stripe; or, if there are, they are ashamed to make a public confession of it. I should be so, too, were I sailing the voyage of life in such a ship. Ask any audience, or any individual, this question, and the result would be the same. What is the inference? Clearly that, if people really do live together who do not love, they are ashamed of it, and, consequently, of the law that holds them; and that they want the world to think that they love each other, and choose to live together on that account, regardless of the law.

Who is there in the community who would like to have it understood that there is no love at home? Isn't it the fact, on the contrary, that those whose homes are loveless, and who fight and wrangle and fuss continually take special pains to conceal these things from the world? Everybody knows it is. What more sweeping condemnation could there be than this, both of the law which compels it and the practice itself? None! It is the hot-bed of hypocrisy, deceit and lust, and is doing more to demoralize the world than all other practices combined.

I am justified, therefore, in concluding that all people who are not practical free lovers, living together for love, are theoretically so, and are ashamed to confess that their practices do not accord with their theories; or, in other words, are ashamed that their practice is enforced lust instead of free love. These are the alternatives, and the only ones, and I don't intend that the people shall escape them. Every one of you—every one of the people generally—either practices Free Love or enforced lust, and the world shall understand when people denounce me as a Free Lover they announce themselves as enforced lusters; and I'll placard their backs and they shall walk up and down the world with this mark of depravity, as they have intended that I should do for having the moral courage, which they lack, to make my theories and practices agree.

There is but one objection, then, to the abolition of this last and greatest of all the slaveries, that, from the popular standpoint, has any validity whatever. This one is the *dernier resort* to which every opposing orator flies when driven from other positions: What will become of the children? Ah! that is the rub, is it? And it is asked with an air of *nonchalance* and self-complacency that seems to say, "Now I have you on the hip." This is the question that everybody asks; but it is not seen that it is answered when the other position is abandoned. The assumption is this: if there were no marriage "the family" would cease to exist, and children would be left on the world. But this preposterous proposition is refuted by the denial and proof that "the family" exists by virtue of law. If the law were abrogated, and men and women should generally live on as now, which they say they would by denying that they live together on account of the law, what would be the difficulty about the children? And yet this bugbear has been pumped up into the imaginations of the people until it is regarded

almost universally as an antidote to all allegations against mar.
riage.

But aside from all this there are direct proofs, equally fatal
to the children antidote. Are there men and women here who,
in the face of this audience, or anywhere else, who, in the face
of any other audience, would dare stand up and confess that
they would abandon their children if the law of marriage were
repealed? I have never been able to find such a person. If
there are such here I want to see them. Barnum would pay a
big price for such animals. I shall never be able to accept the
doctrine of total depravity as app'icable to any person until I
meet such a specimen. The Darwinian order of descent
acknowledges no such connecting link.

Oh, no! Of course WE could never neglect our children
under any circumstances, but we fear that our neighbors might,
therefore it wouldn't be quite expedient to give them an opportunity. If I were to go to your neighbors they would say the
same of you. So the world goes on—one-half of it submitting
to a semblance of law which they really despise, pretending
that it is necessary on their neighbors' account—the old pharisaical godliness, "I am holier than thou," and I thank God
that "I am not as other men are."

If people are really honest, however, in this opinion of
their neighbors they should settle the matter. Let them go to
their neighbors and say, "Now, my friends, here is a law upon
the statute books that is an expensive one to administer, which, so
far as I am concerned, might as well be repealed; but I fear if
it be done that you would abandon your children and perhaps
do a great many other bad things that I, with my superior
honor and manhood, could not stoop to do." My opinion is
that neigbors would help them out of doors much more rapidly
than they entered, especially if there should be heavy boots ready
for service, with this advice gratis, if in the rapidity of the
movement it shouldn't be forgotten: "You had better go home
and take care of your own family, and you won't have so much
time to worry yourself about mine."

It is this stuff that is the matter with the world. Everybody, individually, is ready for freedom, but regards everybody
else, collectively, as being in danger. Everybody is afraid that
everybody else's wife and daughters would go to the bad if
social freedom were to obtain, and their children to the dogs if
the leash of the law were to be let loose. And these are what
are offered as arguments against the introduction of freedom
into the social relations.

It is an imputation that neither you, nor I, nor anybody
else would submit to for a moment were we to consider its inso-
lence. It is an insult alike to the manhood of man and the
womanhood of woman. and an outrage upon good sense and
common decency.

But I would not leave the children question under the

impression that I think their present conditions are by any means what they ought to be. Indeed I believe that they could not well be worse, and that an equally radical revolution is required in the methods of rearing and educating the young as those in begetting them. But right begetting stands first in importance, hence the marriage question is the first one to be revolutionized.

Without going into details, such methods for rearing and educating children should obtain as will give to them the right to live to adult age, each having had equal advantages in all directions with every other child; that shall assure each the capacity and acquirements for good citizenship; and equal pecuniary endowments, so that all may begin adult life equal. Freedom without equality is a fraud; and both these, without justice, a snare. There is but one question to ask: How can children be born, reared and instructed to make them the best men and women, physically, mentally and morally. If the answer demand the abrogation of so-called parental rights and authority they must go. The best interests of children, at whatever cost, is the proper motto. It's useless to waste time upon the present generation. Let it go; but its ignorance and stupid blundering should not be transmitted to the next.

Nor should one-half of all the children born continue to die before reaching the age of five years, sacrificed, as they now are, to the inexcusable ignorance of mothers—murdered, it ought rather to be said, by the popular barbarity which condones ignorance of sexual matters. This fact is a commentary upon our social relations that transforms them into horrid tragedies and stamps the mark of Cain upon every mother. When a ship founders at sea, with the loss of a few hundred lives, the whole world is shocked at the horror; but it sleeps quietly over the still greater horror of double that number of children—babes, almost—falling victims, daily, to these fell destroyers, the so-called safeguards of society, maintained by the canting hypocrisy of its fifty thousand ministerial frauds who know better, and the sham morality and mock-modesty of their willing dupes.

Some time ago, when lecturing in Massachusetts, a lady said: "Do you see that woman at the window opposite, weeping? She buried her daughter to-day—her only child, fourteen years old."

Without thought, I asked, "What was the matter with her?"

She replied, "Can't you imagine—a girl, and fourteen years of age? Last summer I carried one of your papers there, in which there was an article entitled, "Sexual Vice in Children." After I had left, she took the tongs and threw it out of the window. To-day she has buried her only child, because she did not read and follow the advice contained in that article. Six days ago her little daughter arrived at puberty. Ignorant of its meaning and frightened at what she could not understand, she, unknown to her mother, washed out her clothes, and put them on. To-day she is in her grave. Now, Mrs. Woodhull, what is your verdict against that mother?"

I replied, "It is the same that ought to be rendered against every mother in the land who can so criminally neglect the education of her daughters upon so vital a matter as this, whether, as in this instance, it is fatal or not: Murderer!"

Infancy and childhood ought to be the most healthy periods of life; but they are ten times more fatal than any other. Of this sickening fact there can be but one verdict: Cut off at the age of from one day to five years, by maternal ignorance. This is still more evident when we remember that, from the very moment children begin to take care of themselves, the death rate diminishes. Think of these things, and then let it be said, if it can, that the social question ought not to be discussed publicly! Why, there is nothing else worthy to be discussed, so long as this remains unsolved! It should be the topic of conversation at the breakfast table, at dinner, at supper—everywhere—until the whole matter is well understood by everybody.

Will the press dare, hereafter, to condemn me for pressing it upon the attention of parents—for showing them the fearful ignorance and its frightful results? No! not directly; but instead of reporting what I say, so that the public may learn, they will daub me with the feculence of their own thoughts, and say I am vulgar and indecent, and ought to be avoided by everybody; and the too-confiding people will repeat the villainous lies in good faith.

A step beyond marriage as a means to gain sexual relations reaches the relations themselves, their uses and abuses. Here a query arises: Which is the end to be gained? Is it marriage merely, regardless of the character of the relations which it legalizes; or is it proper, natural, healthful, useful relations, such as will bless the parties themselves and the children who result? In other words, is it happiness, and peace, and comfort, and health, and all the good which can follow; or is it the legal union regardless of results?

Let us see. There will scarcely be found in this late day any intelligent person who will maintain that marriage ought ever to be consummated by persons between whom there is no love. The argument is, that men and women who love each other may consummate that love after being legally married but not otherwise; and if either party refuse to consummate the marriage, it becomes void. This establishes the theory that the principal feature of marriage is legal. But this controverts the common consent that love is a necessary precedent. Almost the whole word is in a "mull" over the confusion of ideas caused by the attempt to make these contradictions harmonize—desiring to live out their interior convictions, but fearing to do so lest they incur the legal or social penalty; desiring that their natural instincts and sentiments should be their guides, but fearing to let them lest they be accounted followers of the baser passions.

The law, then, and the real convictions of the people are at variance; but since the latter are inherent in the constitution of man, while the former is a contrivance of his intellect, invented for specific purposes, it must be concluded that the latter ought to take precedence in determining the conduct of life. And when it is remembered that the law binds together only those people who otherwise would separate, this conclusion becomes inevitable.

After careful observation I have deliberately concluded that there are two classes only who have anything more than an imaginary interest in maintaining the marriage system: The hypocritical priests who get their fees for forging the chains and the blackguard lawyers who get bigger ones for breaking the fetters. The former have an average of ten dollars a job, and some of them a hundred jobs a year; while the latter, not quite up to the former in number, to keep even with them, raise their average price per job to two hundred and fifty dollars. A thousand dollars a year for the priests! How should people know whether they ought to marry or not without asking their consent? Of course marriage is divine! A thousand dollars a year for the lawyers! How could people be supposed to know whether they ought to separate or not until the lawyer has got his fee? Of course virtue must have a legal standard. How could morality and modesty be preserved unless the priest got his ten dollars; or how could husbands and wives be prevented from killing each other unless the lawyer got his two hundred and fifty? Will the priest ever cease his cant about the former, or the lawyer change the law about the latter so long as the people are fools enough to pay them fees? They who suppose they may, don't yet understand how much divinity there is in this marriage business.

The real question at issue then is one entirely apart from law, relating wholly to the conditions that make up the unity, whether they are such as judged by the results, warrant the unity that is sought. What are proper and what improper sexual relations is the problem to be solved, and it is that one which of all others is most fraught with the interests, the happiness and the real well-being of humanity. Upon these relations, as I shall show, depend not only the health, happiness and prosperity of the present generation, but the very existence of future generations.

That existence is involved in these relations. If they be pure and good and withal natural, which they must be to be pure and good, then the existence which they make possible will be of the same character; but if they be impure, bad, and withal unnatural, which if they are they must be impure and bad, then the existence which they make possible will be of like character. A pure fountain sends forth pure waters, but

the stream flowing from an impure source will assuredly be un-
clean. To make the fountains of life—the sexual relations—
pure, is the work of the reformer, so that the streams they send
forth may flow through coming ages uncontaminated by any
inherited contagion.

There are a few propositions necessary to be laid down that
will become self-evident as the subject develops : 1. A man or
woman who has perfect physical health, has natural and healthful sexual relations. 2. A man or woman, married or single,
old or young, professional prostitute or *roue*, or a professed
nun or celibate, who has bad general health—and suffers from
any chronic disease—has unnatural and unhealthy sensual conditions. 3. A man and woman, living together, who have perfect physical health, have natural and healthful sexual relations, and will have healthy offspring. Such a union is God-
ordained, if it do not have the approval of the law or the sanction of the priest ; and no man can put it asunder. 4. If either
or both of the parties to a union have generally poor physical
health—suffer from any chronic disease—such parties have unnatural and unhealthful sexual relations, and their progeny will
be puling, weakly, miserable, damned. Such a union is God-
condemned if it have the approval of all the laws, and the blessing of all the priests in the world ; and as corollary to all these,
this : All diseases not to be attributed to so-called accidental
causes are the result of improper, or the want of proper, sexual,
conditions ; and this applies to all ages and to both sexes.

It may now be asked : What are proper sexual conditions !
I reply : Sexual commerce that is based upon reciprocal love and
mutual desire, and that ultimates in equal and mutual benefit,
is proper and healthful ; while improper sexual commerce is
that which is not based upon reciprocal love and mutual desire,
and that cannot, therefore, ultimate in equal or mutual benefit.
Children begotten by the former commerce will never be bad
children physically, mentally or morally ; but such as are begotten by the latter commerce will inevitably be bad children,
either physically, mentally or morally, or, which is more likely
to be the case, partially bad throughout.

I desire to be fully understood upon this part of the subject. I have been generally denounced by the press as an advocate of promiscuousness in the sexual relations. I want you to
fully comprehend the measure of truth there is in this charge.
Hence I repeat that there is but one class of cases where commerce of the sexes is in strict accordance with nature, and that,
in this class, there are always present, First, love of each by each
of the parties ; second, a desire for the commerce on the part of
each, arising from the previous love ; and third, mutual and reciprocal benefit.

Of improper sexual commerce there are several classes :
First, that class where it is claimed by legal right, as in marriage ; second, where the female, to please the male, accords it

without any desire on her own part; third, where, for money, for a home, for any present, as a payment for any claim, whether pecuniary or of gratitude, or for any motive whatever other than love, the female yields it to the male; fourth, where there is mutual love and desire, but where, for any reason, there is such want of adaptation as to make mutual consummation impossible.

This is the promiscuousness that I advocate now, and that I have, from the first, advocated.

Will the representatives of the press, who have covered me with their abuse until I am regarded with horror all over the land as a person whose presence is contamination and whose touch contagion, correct their foul lies by stating these propositions, and, so far as they can at this late day, do me justice? We shall see!

"But," said a prominent woman of this country, with whom I was recently discussing these maxims in sexuality, "how are you going to prevent all this intercourse of the sexes, which you condemn?"

"Ah!" said I, "that's the question. I have no right nor has anybody else any right to prevent it in any such sense as you infer."

This is a matter that must be remanded back from law, back from public inteference, to individuals, who alone have the sovereignty over it. No person or set of persons, however learned and wise, have any right, power or capacity, to determine legally for another when commerce is proper or when it shall occur. It is not a matter of law to be administered by the public, but a question of education to be gained by individuals—a scientific problem to expound and elucidate which, should be one of the chief duties of all teachers and reformers. Every person in the world, before arriving at the age in which the sexual instinct is developed, should be taught all there is known about its uses and abuses, so that he or she shall not ignorantly drift upon the shoals whereon so many lives are wrecked.

I advocate complete freedom for sexuality the same as for religion. The charge of promiscuousness is laid in this fact, and some intelligent minds have thought it was a sound charge, until its inconsistency and utter absurdity have been pointed out to them. This is the proposition: I advocate sexual freedom for all people—freedom for the monogamist to practice monogamy, for the varietist to be a varietist still, for the promiscuous to remain promiscuous. Am I, therefore, an advocate of promiscuousness, variety or monogamy? Not necessarily either. I might do all this and be myself a celibate and an advocate of celibacy. To advocate freedom in sexual things and also the right of individuals to choose each for himself to which class to belong, is by no means synonymous with the advocacy of the class which he chooses. Advocating the right to do a thing and advocating the doing of that thing are two entirely separate and different matters.

Is not this too clear to be misunderstood? I will make it still clearer, lest some may not see it. As I said, I not only advocate sexual freedom, but also religious freedom. I claim that every individual has the right to be a Pagan, Christian, Jew, Mohammedan, Quaker, Oneida Perfectionist, Calvinist, Baptist, Methodist, Trinitarian, Unitarian, Universalist, or whatever else he has a mind or the will to be. Every person advocates the same right—the same freedom—and I am sure if an attempt were made to subvert this right in this country, every hand would be raised against it. I am, however, neither one nor any of these, but a Spiritualist, and I bend all my religious energies to the advocacy of Spiritualism.

Nobody would think of calling me a Romanist because I say that everybody has the right to be a Catholic; but, transfer the question from religion to sexuality, and because I advocate the same theory for this that I do for religion, I am denounced as an advocate of promiscuousness. Did any of you ever hear that I ever said that the monogamist has no right to practice monogamy? Was I ever known to assert that all people should be promiscuous, or varietists? No! What am I, then? I cannot be all of them. Why then class me as promiscuous? I will tell you why: Simply to brand me with supposed infamy, and to frighten the people so that they shall not come to an understanding of these things. That's the reason, and the press knows it.

There is an honest difference of opinion among its advocates in regard to what will be the result of sexual freedom, but none in regard to freedom itself. Some thinkers of wide experience in social matters have concluded that ultimately there will be no constant sexual relation; that change will be the order of society. Others, equally honest and conscientious, believe that a select variety will be the order; while others, still, hold just as firmly that the perfected union of one man and one woman is the highest order. I do not remember ever to have made a speech on this subject in which I did not affirm my belief in the latter order. Not because I desired to soften the feeling against me by so doing, but because I conscientiously believe that in such conditions will be found the highest attainable happiness; and I urge education, discussion and enlightenment upon the subject, believing that they will tend to carry the people toward this condition. Therefore, while I advocate the right of the promiscuously inclined to be promiscuous if they will, I ought to be classed as a monogamist. But if freedom be right in the abstract it does not matter whether monogamy or promiscuousness be the ultimate, since let it be which it may it will be right.

I cannot illustrate the ridiculous ideas of promiscuousness

better than by relating an incident that once happened to me while traveling from Washington to New York. I was approached by an intelligent woman, who, learning who I was, desired to hear my opinions for herself. In the conversation that ensued she remarked, "Oh, Mrs. Woodhull, is it true that you are a promiscuous woman?"

I replied, quietly, "Well, I do not know what you would call promiscuousness. Let me ask you a question, and then I may be able to determine."

Looking her in the face I saw the figure 4 appear upon her forehead. I said, "Madame, I believe you have known at least four different men sexually. Is that true?"

"Oh, yes! I am now living with my fourth husband."

Turning away from her with affected disdain I replied, "Madame, you are altogether too promiscuous for me."

Society permits a woman to have a dozen men, legally, in as many years, and she is all right. She's sound on the Goose Question. But if a woman live with her sexual mate without the payment of the fee, she is all wrong; she is a prostitute. And this is called purity, called morality! I say damn such morals. Such purity stinks. Logically, there is room for no other conclusion than this: That let the highest order of sexuality be what it may, the monogamists have no more right to enforce monogamy by law, as the rule of society, than the promiscuous have to enforce promiscuousness as the order to be observed. Society does, however, attempt to enforce monogamy, but it makes a bad failure.

The Oneida Communists, on the contrary, do not permit monogamic attachments. If they are found springing up, the parties are compelled to separate. If we are to judge which is the better rule by the results, nobody who has ever visited Oneida will hesitate a moment in the decision. Judged by its fruits—by its prosperity, its honesty, its morality, its health— Oneida is the best order of society now on the earth. Its enforced promiscuousness is preferable even to our enforced monogamy, and for very good reasons, which will become evident further on.

Suffice it, here, that promiscuous sexuality among people who have no love attachments, is not so debased a condition as is that which prevails so widely in marriage, where passion in the male, vents itself at the expense of disgust in the female. I know these are bitter pills for those to swallow who think that purity consists in fidelity to marriage. But whether bitter or sweet, they are true; and though I may be cursed now, if they purge the people of their false and absurd notions about sexual purity, I shall some day have their thanks for administering them. I offer you the remedy of Free Love as an antidote for enforced lust, and the world will have to take it before the disease can be cured.

So much for promiscuousness. But what of prostitution,

what of love and what of lust? Terrible words are these in the vocabulary of modern society, but still more so in that of social reform! The question with it is, not as to what is the popular meaning of these terms, but what is their natural, their scientific significance as tested by exact analysis or the stern logic of experience?

Prostitution is popularly applied to certain kinds of sexual commerce? but it has a much wider application, extending to every faculty, function and capacity of the body and mind. It means a perverted, unnatural or excessive use of a capacity. A person who overworks his body or brain is a prostitute. The unhealthy use of anything is its prostitution. They prostitute their stomachs who over-eat or over-drink. Therefore, prostitution, sexually, means a great deal more than intercourse obtained in houses of ill-fame for money. In a scientific sense, it means all sexual commerce that has not a proper basis in love and desire. There may be prostitution in marriage, and proper commerce in the bawdy house. It depends upon the specific conditions attending the act itself, and not where or how it is obtained.

In the exact sense, the woman who sells her body promiscuously is no more a prostitute than she is who sells herself in marriage without love. She is only a different kind of a prostitute. Nor are either of them any more prostitutes than are the countless wives who nightly yield their unwilling bodies to lecherous husbands, whose aim is sexual gratification without regard to the effect upon their victims. The difference is this: In the latter cases the men have legal permission to use the women whether they desire or object, while in the former the woman consults her own wishes—it is a slip of paper costing twenty-five cents and upward, good during life, that a man carries about with him to save the expense of purchasing, from time to time, elsewhere.

It's a sharp trick played by men upon women, by which they acquire the legal right to debauch them without cost, and to make it unnecessary for them to visit professional prostitutes, whose sexual services can only be obtained for money. Now, isn't this true? Men know it is. Those who haven't a wife know very well that they procure for money what they would otherwise have by law. And what is more disgraceful still, is that thousands of men marry because they cannot afford the cost of satisfying their sexual demands with prostitutes. You and I and everybody else know that what I say is true, and yet the sanctity of marriage—the holy sacrament—is talked of as if it had existence! Bosh! It's an insult to common honesty to trade in such stuff and call it holy. Holy! To me it is nastiness; or if there is any worse name, call it that.

I know hundreds of wives who confess privately that they would not live another day with their husbands if they had any other method of support; and yet pass the poor prostitute as though her touch were leprous. As between the two, the legal prostitute is the more depraved at heart. It is axiomatic, that only those women are really pure whose sympathies go out to the unfortunate whom society has driven to the street and brothel by its unjust anathema; who can visit them without contamination; whose virtue is so assured that it is above suspicion. If there is any sister in this place so low that no other woman will visit her, tell me; there will my feet wend their way. If there is any child so wretched that none will care for it, there will my mother's heart wander.

Why should Christian women shun the outcasts of society? The Master whom they profess, habitually made them His companions. What excuse can they offer for a departure from His example? None! But it adds to their long lists of crimes the sin of hypocrisy. Let them beware lest the harlots get into the Kingdom before them.

What a commentary upon the divinity of marriage are the watering places during the summer seasons! The mercenary "mammas" trot out their daughters on exhibition, as though they were so many stud of horses, to be hawked to the highest bidder. It's the man who can pay the most money who is sought; it makes no difference how he got it, nor what are his antecedents. It doesn't matter if he is just from the hands of the physician, cured of a loathsome disease; if he have the cash he is the man. To him who bids highest, in the parlance of the auctioneer, the article is knocked down.

Everybody knows that this is the ruling spirit, not at watering places only, but in so called best society everywhere. Marriages of love become rarer year after year, while those of convenience are proportionately on the increase. How much better is this than the actual exposure and sale, of Oriental practice? Yet we boast of superior intelligence, purity and morals! and we prate of the holy marriage covenant! Verily, we "make clean the outside of the platter, but within are dead men's bones and all uncleanliness."

I respect and honor the needy woman who, to procure food for herself and child, sells her body to some stranger for the necessary money; but for that legal virtue which sells itself for a lifetime for a home, with an abhorrence of the purchaser, and which at the same time says to the former, "I am holier than thou," I have only the supremest contempt. If there is anything that is vulgar it is a modern fashionable marriage. The long retinue, the church, the priest—all to do what? To give the bride, sexually, to the bridegroom. It is a public notice that these people, who have been everything else to each other, are now united sexually. Why, modesty itself should forbid such a parade!

But would you break up that which is called prostitution? The women can do it if they will. The virtuous women of an eastern city recently made an effort. They called secret meetings, and resolved to visit "the houses" and learn who it was that supported them, and then afterward to ostracize them. The visiting began. The New York papers were filled with the matter; day after day column after column was devoted to this crusade. After a week it suddenly stopped. The press was mystified. What was the matter? Had the women succeeded? Nothing could be learned. Finally one of the keenest of the metropolitan Bohemians determined to solve the matter. He visited this inland city; but not a word from the recently zealous women. They said they had abandoned the project; but would give no reason. At last he visited the keepers of the houses, and from them he got the key to the sudden closing of the campaign. "The women," they said, "pressed their investigations until they pressed themselves into the faces of the best men of the city, some of them their husbands and brothers; and considering that they could not ostracize this class of persons they went home and delivered 'Candle Lectures' instead."

Now I will tell you wherein they failed, and why they were not honest. When they found their best men—their husbands and brothers—were supporting these women—consorting with them of course—they should have taken them home and seated them at their tables beside their companion, and said: "If you are good enough for our husbands to consort with, you are good enough to sit at our tables with them, and to occupy their homes with us, and to visit where we visit, and generally to be our companions."

If the women, in every city where there are professional prostitutes, would organize, and agree to bring the women home to the men who visit them, prostitution, so called, would be abolished at once. It is the women who stand in the way. They, knowing that their husbands visit these women, continue to live on, doing their best to damn the women, but saying nothing about the men. They probably forget that the wife who consorts with the man whom she knows consorts with prostitutes, is just as bad as they are.

But where is prostitution in its greatest luxury? At Washington. There are to be found the most elegant mansions, most sumptuously furnished. Why all this magnificence? Why, indeed! Because in Washington there are assembled the best, the most brilliant men in the nation—the men to whom the people have committed the national interests and who conduct the national affairs. Of course there should be all the elegance that wealth can furnish for the accommodation of such men. And there is; of course there ? And they know how to appreciate it, I can assure you.

Everybody knows what the "third house" in Washington is. It consists of the lobbyists who are there to obtain legislation—to push this little scheme, or that small appropriation. Large sums of money are expended by this lobby. When a particular scheme is to come up, its friends distribute ten, fifteen and even twenty thousand dollars among the mistresses of these houses. Why? To secure their influence with Representatives and Senators. You needn't take my word for this; anybody who will inquire can learn the truth. Of course none of these gentlemen ever visit these houses to get under this purchased influence. Oh no! It is exerted upon them by these women magnetically, from afar off, of course it is.

I say it boldly, that it is the best men of the country who support the houses of prostitution. It isn't your young men, but the husbands and fathers of the country, who occupy positions of honor and trust. It is not the hard-working, industrial masses at all, but those who have money and time to expend for such purposes, who are really the old hoary-headed villains of the country. The young haven't money enough to support themselves. So when you condemn the poor women, whom you have helped to drive to such a life, remember to visit your wrath upon the best men of the country as well.

And when legislators discuss Social Evil bills let the women demand equality for their outraged sisters. These bills are professedly to prevent the spread of venereal diseases, and they provide for the medical examination and registration of women to effect it. Now if they really wish to stop these diseases and make the business safe, why not register and examine every man who visits these houses before he is admitted. A house of prostitution, free from disease cannot be contaminated, except through the visits of diseased men. Examine the men, then, and deny admission to the diseased, and there will be an end of the business. How many Social Evil bills would be passed under such conditions? Echo answers, "How many?"

But we are told that prostitution is a "necessary evil," and long articles are published tending to establish this proposition. Necessary for what? So that men may satiate their sexual demands. This is the plain English of it! Mothers, what does this say to you! This, and it is a blotch of infamy upon womanhood that can never be effaced except by woman herself rising in the dignity and divinity of her maternal nature and making a falsity of the damning fact: that you must yearly contribute a certain percentage of your daughters to fill the infernal maw of prostitution; give them up to be sunk in infamy, to be abhorred of their sisters and despised of their brothers: in a word, to walk the prostitutes' road to hell.

Necessary evil! Necessary indeed! Isn't it rather your shame, and my shame, and the dishonor of womanhood and the disgrace of manhood that should make the stones weep to contemplate—a million of innocent, virgin girls of from twelve to sixteen years of age—your daughters, mine, perhaps—sacrificed to this "necessary evil" every fifteen years! Think of it, mothers, and let the blush of shame never fade from your cheeks until this infamy is blotted from existence; or until you have made the victims of this "necessary evil" as respectable as its promoters and supporters.

Statistics inform us that there are two hundred and fifty thousand professional prostitutes in the country, nearly one-tenth of whom are in New York City; and that these are visited and supported by not less than two and a half millions of men —one-third of the voting population of the country. Think of it! A quarter of a million professional female prostitutes and two and a half millions of professional male prostitutes, or ten men to one woman. And yet Congress is wonderfully concerned about Utah. Consistency is a jewel which Congressmen don't seem to carry about with them. They must be jealous of the Mormons. If the proportions were reversed so that there would be ten women to one man on their side of the question, they would probably let Brigham alone, and think it rather a nice thing to be a Mormon ; but Brigham has got the better of them; 'twas very wicked of him to go and do such a thing ; very, very wicked that he should, in a small way, presume to imitate both the meekest and the wisest of the Biblical fathers.

But love and lust are terms equally misapplied even by the most brilliant minds. Love is an universal principle. It is the life of the universe. It is that power called attraction which holds all things together. It is that force which unites the two elements from which water is formed and the two natures of which a sexual unit is composed. It uplifts the mountains and depresses the valleys ; causes the water to flow and the clouds to float; the lily to blossom and the violet to bloom ; the dew to fall and the storm to descend ; it is the living and motive power of the world ; it is God.

The Christian tells the same story, but he speaks in a language which he does not understand—God is Love. If this be so, then Love is God ; then all the love there is, is God ; but this love they tell us is free. I have been endeavoring to convince them of the truth of their own most cherished, though heretofore meaningless proverb, so that they may appreciate its beauty and bask in its glory, and for my pains I am dubbed "the Devil." I have tried to show that all love must be as they say that God is—Free ; that love cannot be confined to the limits of a man-made law any more than God can be shut up in a creed. Attempt to put the limits of a written law about love, saying, thus far and no farther, and love is destroyed. It is no longer love, because it is limited, and love, being God, cannot be limited.

When a limit is placed upon anything that by nature is free, its action becomes perverted. All the various attractions in the world are but so many methods by which love manifests itself. The attraction which draws the opposites in sex together is sexual love. The perverted action of sexual love, when limited by law or otherwise, is lust. All sexual manifestations that are not free are the perverted action of love—are lust. So, logically, the methods enforced by man to ensure purity convert love into lust. Legal sexuality is enforced lust. All the D. D.'s and LL. D.'s in the world, though they have all the mental gifts and the tongues of angels, cannot controvert the proposition.

This brings us to a still more serious part of my subject. Remember I am to withhold nothing—no fact, no advice. We are now face to face with the most startling and the most common fact connected with the miseries of marriage. But I know of no author, no speaker who has dared to call attention to, or to suggest a remedy for it, or even to hint at it as needing a remedy, or to recognize its existence in any manner.

It will be remembered that early in the evening I showed that marriage when analyzed, is a license to cohabit sexually. Now I am going to show that the enforcement of this method eventually defeats the original object. I state it without fear of contradiction by fact or of refutation by argument that it is the common experience among the married who have lived together strictly according to the marriage covenant, for from five to ten years, that they are sexually estranged. There may be, I know there are, exceptions to this rule, but they are the exceptions and not the rule. It is a lamentable fact that all over this country there is a prolonged wail going up on account of this condition. Sexual estrangement in from five to ten years! Think of it, men and women whom Nature has blessed with such possibilities for happiness as are conferred on no other order of creation—your God-ordained capacity blasted, prostituted to death, by enforced sexual relations where there is neither attraction or sexual adaptation; and by ignorance of sexual science!

Some may assert, as many do, that failure in sexual strength is intellectual and spiritual gain. Don't harbor the unnatural lie. Sexuality is the physiological basis of character and must be preserved as its balance and perfection. To kill out the sexual instinct by any unnatural practice or repression, is to emasculate character; is to take away that which makes what remains impotent for good—fruitless, not less intellectually and spiritually than sexually.

It is to do even more than this. From the moment that the sexual instinct is dead in any person, male or female, from that moment such person begins actually to die. It is the fountain from which life proceeds. Dry up the fountain and the stream will disappear. It is only a question of time, and of how much is obtained from other fountains, when the stream will discharge its last waters into the great ocean of life.

Others again seem to glory over the fact that they never had any sexual desire, and to think that this desire is vulgar. What! Vulgar! The instinct that creates immortal souls vulgar! Who dare stand up amid Nature, all prolific and beautiful, whose pulses are ever bounding with the creative desire, and utter such sacrilege! Vulgar, indeed! Vulgar, rather, must be the mind that can conceive such blasphemy. No sexual passion, say you? Say, rather, a sexual idiot, and confess that your life is a failure, your body an abortion, and no longer bind your shame upon your brow or herald it as purity. Call such stuff purity. Bah! Be honest, rather, and say it is depravity.

It is not the possession of strong sexual powers that is to be deprecated. They are that necessary part of human character which is never lacking in those who leave their names standing high in the historic roll. The intellect, largely developed, without a strong animal basis is never prolific of good in any direction. Evenly balanced natures, in which there are equal development and activity of all departments are those which move the world palpably forward for good; but if superiority of any kind is desirable at all, let it be in the animal, since with this right, the others may be cultivated to its standard. If this be wanting, however, all possible cultivation, intellectually, will only carry the individual further away from balance, and make the character still more "out of tune" with nature. These are physiological facts inherent in the constitution of mankind, and they cannot be ignored with impunity. No reliable theory of progressive civilization can ever be established that does not make them its chief corner stone, because they are the foundation upon which civilization rests.

It is the misuse, the abuse, the prostitution of the sexual instinct that is to be deprecated. Like all other capacities, it needs to be educated, cultivated, exercised rightly, and to do this is to live in accordance with nature and as commanded by the higher law, that law which every one finds deep-seated in his soul, and whose voice is the truest guide. When the world shall rise from its degradation into the sphere of this law, when the sexual act shall be the religion of the world, as it is now my religion, then, and then only, may we reasonably hope that its redemption is nigh.

What other religion so near alike to God—the all-loving, all-creating Father; or so much in harmony with Nature—the ever-receptive and ever-evolving Mother. Let your religious faith be what it may if it do not include the sexual act it is impotent. Make that act the most divine of all your worship. Let it be unto you without spot or blemish. Let it rise unto God a continual incense of piety and holiness, and be henceforth resurrected from the debauch in which the ages have sunk it. This is my religion—the fundamental principles for the generation of the race. Let it be yours and all mankind's, and with no other, the salvation long sought, long prayed for, long prophesied and long sung will soon be found. Discard it, put its life and health-giving blessings aside, and all the other religions ever conceived or dreamed, or that may be conceived of dreamed, combined, will be impotent to usher in the glad time.

Oh! that my lips were smitten with the inspiration of an archangel, that I might reach your hearts and show you the better life; that I might pierce your understandings and force in upon them the mighty import of these truths. Oh! that I could so appeal to my brothers everywhere, that forever after they would regard women as of angelic order, to be approached only as they would approach the enthroned Goddess of Purity. upon whose presence none would dare presume, and whose favors it is theirs to merit and receive, rather than to command and appropriate. Look not upon her for selfish purposes, but rather to bless her, let that blessing depend upon what it may. even if to bless is not to possess. Other love than this is selfishness, and a profanation of the Holy Word. That is love which will bless the object, even if to do so is to yield it. Remember that it is a pretension and a fraud to think of ownership in, or control over, the person of a woman. This is her inheritance, never to be bartered, never to be sold, never to be given away, even; but only to be exchanged, blessing for blessing, when an all-absorbing, all-embracing, all-desiring love points out the way.

And my sisters. Oh! what shall I say to them; how awaken them to realize the awful responsibilities conferred through their maternal functions. How shall I arouse, how startle them into a comprehension of the divinity of maternity: how sting them, if nothing else will do it, into self-respect? How shall I show them the destruction they have sown broadcast over the earth; how exhibit the black damnation, the sin, misery, shame, crime, disgrace, that come home to them as mothers; how stab their hearts with the awful monstrosities with which they have desecrated the earth; how bring to their hearts, to wring them in bitter anguish, the wild ravings of the maniac, the senseless drivel of the chattering idiot, the horrid delirium of the drunkard, the desolate moans of the "outcasts," the heart-sobs of criminals, the dreaded spectacle of the murderer, face to face with death? Ah! how adequately shall I bring these things—all these—home to the mothers of humanity; how make them feel the horrid misery that they have wrought by the outrage and desecration of their divine maternal functions?

Oh! mothers, that I could make you feel these things as I know them. I do not appeal to you as a novice, ignorant of what I speak, merely to excite your sympathies, but as one having learned through long years of bitter experience. Go where I have been; visit the prisons, insane asylums and the glittering hells that I have visited; see the maniac mother at the cell door of her son, to be hanged in the morning, as I have seen her—cursing God, cursing man, cursing until nothing but curses filled the air, and until their fury flecked her face with foam, that her crime should be visited upon her poor, poor boy. Follow her home, and when the agony of the gallows has come and gone, ask her the meaning of all this, and she will tell you, as she has told me: "That boy was forced upon me; I did not want him; I was worn out by child-bearing; and I tried, in every way I knew, to kill him in my womb. I thought of nothing else until it was too late to think of that. I failed. He was born; and I have made him a murderer. He committed the deed, and has suffered an ignominious death; but I am the real criminal.

"But I did not do this willfully. I had never been taught any better—never been told the fearful effect of such acts and deeds upon the unborn child. I followed the common practices of my friends. I did not know I was stamping my child with the brand of Cain. But all this did not save him. He was hanged for my crime."

But look upon another scene. Go home with me and see desolation and devastation in another form. The cold, iron bolt has entered my heart and left my life a blank, in ashes upon my lips. Wherever I go I carry a living corpse in my breast, the vacant stare of whose living counterpart meets me at the door of my home. My boy, now nineteen years of age, who should have been my pride and my joy, has never been blessed by the dawning of reasoning. I was married at fourteen, ignorant of every thing that related to my maternal functions. For this ignorance, and because I knew no better than to surrender my maternal functions to a drunken man, I am cursed with this living death. Do you think my mother's heart does not yearn for the love of my boy? Do you think I do not realize the awful condition to which I have consigned him? Do you think I would not willingly give my life to make him what he has a right to be? Do you think his face is not ever before me pressing me on to declare these terrible social laws to the world? Do you think with this sorrow seated on my soul I can ever sit quietly down and permit women to go on ignorantly repeating my crime? Do you think I can ever cease to hurl the bitterest imprecations against the accursed thing that has made my life one long misery? Do you think I can ever hesitate to warn the young maidens against my fate, or to advise them never to surrender the control of their maternal functions to any man! Ah! if you do, you do not know the agony that rests here. Not to do less than I am doing were madness; it were worse than crime; it were the essence of ten thousand crimes concentrated in one soul to sink it in eternal infamy.

Nor is this all that urges me onward. A few months ago I laid a beautiful sister away in Greenwood. Above her is written, "Cut off by marriage at thirty-one years." She had always opposed my social theories, though I knew her life was being sacrificed to a legal marriage. When on her death-bed she called me to her and said, "My darling sister, I am going to die. Oh! if I could have had the moral courage to have stood by you and to have broken loose from my thralldom I should not have been here. I knew you were right; but I could not endure the obloquy that the ungrateful world was heaping upon you. Knowing that I am to die I wanted to see you alone and ask your forgiveness for the anguish I have caused you by joining with the world to crush you out. It is meet that I should be sacrificed. I deserve it. It is just. But I shall soon be freed from the galling chains I dared not break myself, and will then be near you to make you bold and strong, and in so far as I can, repair the injury I have done."

My brothers and sisters, I never walk upon a platform without feeling the presence of that darling sister; and I now see her beautiful face flitting above me, hear her sweet voice encouraging me, and feel her magnetic power inspiring me to do my duty. "Cut off by marriage at thirty-one" rings in my ears, and I repeat it to the world as the mournful refrain of millions of wives, who, like her, were its victims; who, like her, after suffering untold miseries for years, went down to untimely graves murdered by the men to whom marriage sold them sexually.

When I review the conditions under which humanity is born I am surprised, not so much that it is so bad, but that it is so good. I do not wonder that there are all classes of criminals, that there are all sorts of diseases, that there are all grades of intellect; I do not wonder that debauchery and drunkenness meet us at every hand, and that lust in adults and sexual vice in children are sapping the life of the people; nor that in summing them all up and calculating their effects that the conclusion is reached that unless there soon come a change the American people will be blotted out. And then tell me that I shall not discuss the sexual question! I should like to see the power or law that can prevent me.

You remember that little game was tried in New York, and failed. When I published the biography of the American Pope, the United States authorities, urged on by the minions of the Church—the Y. M. C. Assassination Association—swooped down upon me and carried me off to jail, not for libel on the Pope, but for obscenity. I remained there quietly enough for some weeks, trusting that the outrage upon the freedom of the press and free speech would rouse the people to my defense against such an unwarrantable act. But Beecher was bigger than a free press—of more consequence than free speech. His danger cowed the whole country into silence; and the people sneaked after the trail of the popular preacher, in abject submission. "It was well worth the while of the United States to protect the reputation of a revered citizen," said District-Attorney Noah Davis; and the whole country complacently repeated it.

What was a little woman, in jail, compared with Mr. Beecher! What if a free press and free speech were imprisoned

with her—were struck down in her person ! What were they to
the American people when Mr. Beecher was in danger; and
through him the whole rascally set of fifty thousand preachers ;
and, through them, again, the Christian Church everywhere !
If she were to rot in jail, what was that beside the necessity
of "hushing things up;" of strangling the scandal before it
should spread into other churches all over the country and
show them all rotten ? Simply nothing.

It was the United States that held me illegally imprisoned.
It was the people everywhere, you among the rest. But you
did not raise a single voice at the outrage. You left me power-
less in the cell of the State while the Church carried the key.
But if you were dead to the infamy, I was not. I saw it was
useless to wait for the people to protest, so I gave battle alone.
I went into the combat single-handed against both Church and
State led on by all their minions, and with the aid of honest
Judge Blatchford, I whipped the whole cowardly crowd. I will
speak what I will ; and I will publish the truth about any professional hypocrite when I think I can render the world a service by so doing. I have just come from a second fight with
them. In the first it was free press and free speech, that triumphed. In the second it was Free Love, and the victory in
both instances was complete. I don't think they will try it over
again ; but if they do, I'll fight them again, armed with truth
and with justice, and have no fears for the result.

But to return from this digression, let us inquire the real
end to be gained by reform. The pretense of every reform ever
advanced has been to better the condition of the people. But
first and last—one and all—they have dealt with existing conditions—with effects—endeavoring to mitigate and cure evils, instead of preventing them. No sooner is one evil cured than the
causes that produced it send forth another that requires to be
cured ; and thus reform, traveling in circles, has made but
little real advance, except in the direction of intellectual development, in which a different practice has prevailed. People are
better, intellectually, than they were ; but not so physically or
morally.

There can be a better race only by having better children.
If they are bad, good men and women are impossible. There
can be better children only through better conditions of generation ; a better understanding by women of the processes of gestation, and better methods of rearing and education. These
propositions are self-evident, and point directly to the sexual
relations as the place to begin the work of improving the race.
All effects in other directions, however promising, will prove fu-
tile for permanent good. The necessity for regeneration must
be replaced by proper generation. If all women in the country
were to join the temperance crusaders they might, for the time,
decrease drunkenness ; but the moment they should cease their
efforts it would return. Now let these women go home and

breed no more drunkards, and the remedy will be effectual. And so of all other vices and crimes.

Not long ago, when passing through Janesville, Wisconsin, a young man who had heard me lecture about the pre-natal effect of the mother's conduct upon the child, came and asked me to look at his breast. I did so. It was covered with bottles. When his mother was carrying him she was in the habit of going into her uncle's liquor store and tasting his liquor. The result was she "marked" him with bottles. Of course this young man is a confirmed drunkard. He might be importuned into signing the pledge a hundred times, but he would always break it at the first opportunity. And what is true of him is also true of nearly every other drunkard. They are made so by their mothers, or else they inherit it from their fathers. The temperance crusade, then, must begin in the home, in the marriage bed, in begetting children, and in proper surroundings and influences for the mother during gestation. Nothing else will ever cure the world of drunkenness, or any other vice.

The power of the mother over the unborn child, for evil, is too well attested by too many facts to need further elucidation. But it teaches a lesson of mighty import which ought to receive universal consideration. If her powers for ill are so marked, what must they be for good, when exercised under an enlightened understanding! Nothing is more certain than that mothers can make their children just what they want them to be, limited only by the inherited tendencies of the father.

There are, then, but two questions in this whole matter of reforming the world; but they are vital and inseparable. The first is, to discover and develop the science of proper generation, so that all the inherited tendencies may be good; and the second is, that the germ life, once properly begun, may not be subjected to any deleterious influences, either during the period of gestation or development on to adult age.

This is the meaning of social reform. It means better children, and it doesn't care how they are to be obtained—only to obtain them. Any methods that will secure them are good, are true, are pure, are virtuous methods. The question to be asked of the mothers of the future will not be, "Who is the father?" but, "How good is the child?" If it be not good it will be a disgrace to the mother, no matter if the father is her legal husband.

I say it, and I want the world to know that I say it, that a woman who bears a dozen or less scraggy, scrawny, puny, half-made-up children, by a legal father, is a disgrace to her sex and a curse to the community; while she who bears as many perfect specimens of humanity, no matter if it be by as many different fathers is an honor to womanhood and a blessing to the world. And I defy both the priests and the law to prove this false.

Every sensible man and woman will have to admit it. It is a self-evident proposition.

In August, 1873, at the Silver Lake camp meeting, I said, before fifteen thousand persons, that no one knows who his father is. Think of it for a moment, and you will see how impossible it is that he should know. Can any person make oath that he knows who it was who, in unity with his mother, was his father? He may swear that he has been told so, but that does not amount to knowledge. I made this statement, not specially to declare this fact, but to enforce the argument that it doesn't make any difference who may be the father of any child, if he is only a good child and an honor to his mother. I have repeated this statement a hundred times since, and never a hiss. Hasn't the sexual question grappled with the thoughts of the people? This is an evidence not to be misunderstood.

But among all the radical things I have never quite equaled one recently published in *The Popular Science Monthly*, in an article written by Mr. Herbert Spencer, the acknowledged philosopher of the age. Quoting from an eminent English surgeon, he says: "It is a lamentable truth that the troubles which respectable, hard-working married women undergo are more trying to the health and detrimental to the looks than any of the irregularities of the harlot's career." What a commentary is this on the marriage institution! Much the larger part of the married women of the world in a worse condition, as to health and looks, than are the harlots! Take that home with you, and think of it, and see if you can come to any other conclusion than that an institution that produces such results in women, needs to be replaced by something better. Now don't forget that these are not my words, and say that I advocate prostitution; but remember that they are the words of the highest authority in philosophy and science now living, published in the most popular monthly in the country, and give them weight accordingly.

There are many popular fallacies about prostitution. Statistics inform us that the average life of prostitutes is about four years; but this does not show the real causes of such fatality. It leaves it to be inferred that it is in the fact of prostitution merely. It does not say that it is caused by dissolute living, and drinking, and by the diseases which usually accompany promiscuous intercourse.

The real truth about this is that those prostitutes who never drink, and who never permit themselves to become diseased are among the healthiest of women, and hold their beauty and vigor to an advanced age. Is this a startling assertion? Anybody who will take the trouble can easily confirm it. I do not make it without the most unmistakable proof, which is open to all inquirers, as it was to me, to obtain. It was necessary for me to know by personal investigation, and it shows me as it will everybody else that what Herbert Spencer writes in *The Pop-*

ular Science Monthly is true : that the promiscuous life of the harlot is less detrimental to health and beauty than is the common life of the married slave. The reason is simple and clear. Promiscuous intercourse, when sexual conditions are imperfect, when the act is not based on mutual love and desire, is better than so-called monogamic intercourse under the same conditions, made more intolerable by a deep-seated disgust. But by no means is this an argument against monogamy. It is an argument against legal monogamy when the monogamy of nature is wanting; and, as such, is the most convincing that can be offered in favor of monogamy founded upon love. Free relations of any kind are better than any can be that are enforced These are the logical deductions from the facts. I did not create the facts, so if you have fault to find, find it with them and not me. I merely offer them to you for consideration, so that you may think of and discuss this subject understandingly.

I have already said that the salvation of the world can come only through better children. This fact has been widely recognized by all so-called Christian denominations. Each is very anxious to get hold of the children. The Romanist says: "Give me the children for twenty-five years and I will make the world Catholic." True enough. They have taken a step in the right direction, but only a step. They say : give me the children, good or bad. The reformer, who shall really save the world, must go another step and see that there are none but good children born. Then the root of the matter will be reached.

But how to accomplish this is now the vital question. Many may think that I am too severe on my sex—on the mothers ; but I wish I could be ten times more so, because, and I say it in sorrow, this is a work for the mothers, to the fearful importance of which I fear they cannot be roused. They have a terrible responsibility resting upon them and a fearful preliminary task to perform. They have got first to conquer their sexual liberty, so that their maternal functions shall be under their own control at all times ; and next to guard them from contamination, so that their children may be pure.

I do not complain of women as willfully sending the race onward to destruction, I only wish to show them that they are doing it, and to urge them by every argument that my woman's nature can suggest, or my mother's heart conceive, to stop the desolation. What can I say? How shall I plead with them to reach their hearts and rouse them into consciousness upon this terrible theme? Shall I remind them again of the death of one half of their children? Shall I show them the still-born babes, strangled at birth because they are not wanted? Shall I tell them that the birth-rate among the more intelligent classes has decreased one-half in twenty years by abortions ; and that, unless these things cease, the race will ultimately be blotted out?

Or shall I turn to the other side of the picture and show. them the awful fact that nine women in ten are so diseased, sexually, as to make them unfit to become mothers, brought to this condition by their efforts to prevent pregnancy, or to procure abortions, or by continually submitting to undesired intercourse until the sexual instinct is dead ; and that if these conditions go on for twenty years it will be impossible for women even to become pregnant?

Or, again, shall I ask them to look on the faces of their children and see the history of sexual vice indelibly written— their boys and their girls, the former in the first stages of self-abuse, or, having too late discovered their danger, in the last stages of spermatorrhea ; and the latter, pale, yellow and dejected from irregularities, or, having too late discovered their cause, prostrated by leucorrhœa and prolapsus uteri?

And having done this, shall I ask them if they wonder that these things are so, when they remember that they were constantly debauched by the insatiable lust of their husbands during the whole period in which they were bearing these children beneath their hearts? What else can be expected than premature and precocious development of the sexual passions in children when, during their gestation, the influence of this passion is continually forced upon them; or what else than that this passion should be vented in vicious ways which carry their victims down to certain destruction?

Or what other pictures can I bring to lay at the feet of mothers to show them the horrors they are working for humanity by this willing sexual slavery in which they slumber as if nothing were the matter? Oh! let me plead with mothers in the name of future generations to rescue your divinely ordered maternity from the horrid debauch in which it is plunged. Let me implore you for your own soul's future happiness to emancipate yourselves, at whatever cost, from the awful crime of sexual slavery, so that you may dedicate your lives to the good of future generations rather than to expend them in ministering to the lustful demands of legal masters. Let me urge upon you, for your own sakes, the strict observance of the laws of your sexual natures, and to never permit their divine instincts to be trifled with or debauched by any man, whether he be husband or lover. Let me beg of you, for humanity's sake, to rescue yourselves from this thralldom of license, snatch yourselves from the rude grasp of lust, and elevate yourselves from the quagmire of disgust into which license and lust have cast you, so that womanhood may once more become Queen of purity, nobility and virtue.

Instead of supporting churches and sending missionaries to the heathen ; of praying and singing to convert the liquor-sellers ; of building and supporting hospitals for foundlings and for women about to become illegal mothers ; of erecting penitentiaries, insane asylums, alms-houses and gallows, let the women come together in solemn conclave and register an eternal vow that they will never bear any more children to fill these places. Let them swear by the God of humanity that they will never again become pregnant of an undesired child. Let them enter a solemn oath that they will never again surrender their sexual or maternal functions to be outraged by undesired commerce. Let the women come together and do these things in earnest and the world will be saved from that time.

I repeat that I do not complain of women as willful perpetrators of all these crimes; but I charge it home upon the intelligent men, upon the teachers, preachers, and doctors especially, that they willfully keep the rest of the world in ignorance of the truths about sexual debauchery. But still more specially do I hurl this indictment against the editors. They know these truths, but they know also if women generally come to a knowledge of them that the sexual domination of man will cease. Hence by blackguarding me they hope to frighten the women away, so that I may not reach their ears. But, thank heaven, they cannot entirely shut them out. Some there are who, having suffered, and knowing there is something wrong somewhere, have the moral courage to come for the facts, and they go away and repeat them to others, until there is a general inquiry among women all over the country to offset this attempt at suppression on the part of men. Some papers also dare sometimes to hint at the facts; sometimes publishing what I say, but taking care to condemn me editorially, so as to make the editorial censure wash the reportorial facts.

The scientific journals and monthlies are filled with articles leading directly to the solution of this question where ten years ago there was not so much as a word to be seen in any publication about sexual subjects, even hinting in the remotest manner that there was anything rotten sexually. If I do nothing else I know that I have awakened investigation on this subject. If all I have said is error; if the truth lie in altogether different directions from those in which I point, out of the discussion now going on the truth will be evolved.

But what is more surprising to me than everything else is that the Chicago *Times*—a paper in which I have been perhaps more vilely abused than in any other—in its issue of April 5th, published, editorially, the following statement: "Could society by some omnipotent fiat determine that, from to-day no sexual intercourse should occur, save in cases where there is a *mens sana in corpore sana* (meaning sound minds in sound bodies) less than half a century hence would witness the closing of hospitals, saloons, penitentiaries and 'houses;' the extinction, almost to a man, of physicians; and the cessation of nearly every movement whose purpose is the lessening of human suffering and vice. Taxes would sink to the minimum; men and women would tread the earth with the springy, buoyant step of perfect health; and the millennium would commence its glorious reign upon this our sin-bestridden and disease-cursed earth." I have never said more than this. If you will not listen to my pleading, accept those of the most influential and widely-circulated journal of the great North-West, and I will rest content to let it speak for me.

Now can you understand for what I have been made the victim of such vile abuse? The truths which I have presented to you are those I have always sought to enforce. I have always contended that, if there is to be any ostracism for prostitution, the men should suffer equally with the women; that the seducer should be held up to the same scorn and contempt that is visited upon the seduced. I have asked for equality—nothing more; and I will accept nothing less for my sex, let them heap whatever contumely they may upon me.

It would appear from their opposition that women do not want the ostracism of male prostitutes, or to be deprived of them as companions; that they do not want the seducer debarred from their society, and he is usually a "lion" among them; that they do not want to own and control their maternal functions and sexual instincts; that they do not want to have the right to say when they shall bear children and when not; but, on the contrary, that they want to be owned, want to be supported by men, in return for the sexual favors which they can confer. They don't want reform; they want things to remain as they are.

Isn't this a legitimate conclusion? Think of it, women of the nineteenth century! Shall your names go down to posterity in such connection? Let me warn you this is where they are going. In September, 1872, I said, before a convention in Boston: I believed that, in twenty years, the daughters of to-day, then grown, would regard their mothers as having been the real prostitutes of this time. If what I have presented are facts, wouldn't it be a just verdict?

A popular objection against Free Love is, that it breaks up families. My answer to this indictment is, that a family which falls in pieces when Free Love strikes it, is already broken up, and waiting for a loophole out of which to escape; and as the press have coupled my name with this *role*, the discontented think it a good thing to shift whatever opprobrium there may be connected with their cases, upon Woodhull. Thus I become the pack-horse for thousands who have no more conception of Free Love than a donkey has of mathematics.

But I'll tell you what I do. If a husband or a wife get discontented and uneasy, and chafe in their bonds, I advise such to seek out the ulcers, come to a mutual understanding, talk out the hidden and corroding cause, sum up the difficulties and grievances and see if they are of such character and magnitude as to preclude all hope for peace and happiness, and not under any circumstances call in the services of a blackguard lawyer.

I ask men and women to be honest with each other. If any

find their attachments growing cold—their love waning—say so, and not continue the pretense while the real love is lavished elsewhere. I ask men and women to be thoughtful of each other's needs and desires. If a wife find her husband spending his evenings away from home, let her be sure there is something wrong; and when he goes again, put on hat and shawl and accompany him. If it is to the club, the bar-room, the billiard table, the theatre, the opera or the house of ill-fame, tell him that any place which he frequents is good enough for you to visit. Face him in his discontent, and say: "What is the matter, my darling? What is it in which I fail that you must spend your evenings away from me? Has your love for me gone, or what is the matter? Tell me? It is useless to continue an unhappy life when there is so easy a remedy. If you do not love me any longer, take me into your confidence; let me be your friend and adviser."

If there is any basis of hope left, this course will develop it; and there are hundreds of families who owe their present unity and happiness to having followed it. It is an error into which people naturally fall who think that my supporters are among the dissatisfied families. It is precisely the reverse of this. It is the families which cannot be separated or broken up which believe in the efficacy of freedom as a regulative element. My most bitter opponents among my own sex, are the professional prostitutes who know I am going to break up their business, and the ignorant wives who read little and think less, and who are in constant fear of losing their "Paw," over whom they have none except a legal control; and among the opposite sex, those who are habitually unfaithful to marriage, and the ministers who know their nice arrangements will be spoiled, and the lawyers, whose divorce business will be ruined by freedom. Ask any of these, when found denouncing Mrs. Woodhull, if they ever heard her speak, or ever read her paper or speeches, the reply will be, "No! and I don't want to."

But I would remind these exceedingly virtuous people that the Catholic says, that every one who was not married by the Catholic method is living in prostitution. So please remember when they cast their epithets about so freely, that there is a greater authority than they are, which denounces them in equally opprobrious terms. This class say that those living together who are not married as they are, are prostitutes; the Catholic Church looks at them, and, because they are not married as it marries, calls them by the same name.

For my part I look beyond the ceremony and the law, and observe the facts; and if I find people living together in hate and disgust, whether married after the Protestant fashion or the Catholic style, I say they are prostituting their sexual functions, and in sight of the God of Nature are prostitutes.

Let us consider briefly the doctrine of stirpiculture, hinted at in the *Times* quotation. Nobody, more than I, feels the need of scientific propagation ; but there is something in men and women of which science can neither take cognizance or control. Men and women are more than animals ; and this additional quantity must be recognized in any successful theory about this matter. Stirpiculture, popularly understood, means that the best men and women, physically, produce the best children. This theory may be, and doubtless is, true as applied to animals ; but observation does not bear out its truth among men and women. Many physically perfect men and women bear bad children. With them, the theory as stated needs to be supplemented as follows : Provided love exists between them.

Women cannot bear their best children except by the men they love best and for whom they have the keenest desire. If these are for the best men, physically, so much the better. There are instances where the husband or the wife, and some, where both, from inherited causes, have bad health, who rear families of robust children ; but in these cases there is a sexual unity which exalts the creative act far above the possibility of inherited contagion ; while others whose children should apparently rank high, physically and mentally, are remarkably deficient in both regards. Nothing is more common than mediocre children in families representing the intellect and morality of the age ; nor the brightest gems where none would think of finding them.

These facts are too common to be ignored ; and they lead unerringly to the conclusion that this science, as applied to animals, cannot be practiced by men and women. It would find an insuperable argument in the repugnance which exists instinctively in women against consorting with men for whom they have no love. Women would revolt against such a theory, and the disgust that would accompany its practice would have a deleterious influence upon the intended result far outweighing any benefit that might be anticipated from mere physical perfection. This alone is a fatal objection, and makes it necessary that other considerations should enter any successful theory for the scientific breeding of humanity.

But of what use is it to talk of stirpiculture while marriage exists ? The very first necessity is freedom for woman, sexually. What can a woman do with a theory so long as she belongs, legally, to any man ? It is preposterous to think of it. Argue stirpiculture to a woman who is compelled to submit herself, sexually, to a legal master whenever he demands it, even to the extent of brutality ! It is simply nonsense. Talk of scientific propagation to a woman bound to a man whose system is loaded with venereal, scrofula or other loathsome disease ! It is absurd. Present any theory of sexual intercourse for the observance of women, so long as they have no control over their maternal functions ! It is insanity. When men do not and will not respect either the wishes or desires of their wives, or the remittant bodily conditions peculiar to women, nor their physical health, however bad it may be—of what use is it to offer women a theory to regulate reproduction! Better spend breath asking the sun to stand still or the moon to visit the earth, than commit the absurdity of offering stirpiculture to married women.

When any of the old-fashioned religious denominations have revivals, they extend a general invitation to sinners to come forward and relate their experiences and be converted; to tell how bad they were before they were better. If this is a good thing to do religiously, why would it not be equally good socially? I'll take the first six married women anywhere, and if they are forced to tell the whole truth about their sexual experience, there would be no further argument necessary to prove that it's idle to talk of stirpiculture so long as women do not own and control their sexual organs; therefore, the first thing for women to do. is to declare themselves free; to assert their individual sovereignty sexually. Until they have the moral courage to do this, and therefore to rescue themselves from prostitution, stirpiculture will do for those to play with who dare not touch the main question.

I have been shown, instinctively, as you would call it, clair voyantly as I would say, the solution of this whole matter; but have not yet been able to reason it out so as to demonstrate it logically. But when impregnation takes place under perfect conditions of love and desire and their mutual consummation, the same process occurs regarding physical impurities as related to the new germ life, that takes place when water is changed to ice. For instance, ice formed from salt water is not salt ice. Salt is a foreign substance to water, and in its natural changes is cast off. So impurities of the human system are foreign substances which, in perfected sexual conditions, form no part of the transmitted qualities. These conditions are to be found only where there is that perfect sexual exaltation which blends two beings in one—"two souls with but a single thought, two hearts that beat as one." that thought and beat being to reproduce their counterpart. Into such an act, no impurity can enter. It is God's sublimest creative impulse; and he who can think of it except in reverence, awe and gratitude, is unfit to enter its sacred chambers. Who can think of its wonders and beauties; its bliss and its holiness, and not worship Him who hath given such possibilities to man !

If this be so, and I feel I know it is, the doctrine of heredity and transmission will have to be remodeled, or rather abandoned, and the solution sought by them obtained in the science of sexuality—which is the science of life. I am the more inclined to this theory from the fact that some men, while sexually poisonous to some women, are a life-giving element to others. The private histories of the divorced and remarried, offer many facts of this kind, and they must form a part of any basis upon which a sexual science can be built.

I should be glad to follow stirpiculture further, but I must leave it by making these propositions, which to me are self-evident:

First—The highest order of humanity results from sexual relations in which love and desire are the only elements present.

Second—The lowest order of humanity results from sexual relations where there is disgust instead of delight, and endurance instead of reciprocity.

Third—The intermediate orders of humanity result from various modifications of these two extremes.

What then is to be inferred from all this, is the purity at which I aim, and to which sexual freedom, as I believe and teach it, will lead. Can any who have heard me, conceive that what I have said tends toward greater sexual debauchery and degradation than now exists? If there are any such they have misconceived the natural tendency of freedom. To pretend to believe that the giving of freedom to woman will plunge her deeper in vice, is to insult all womanhood; it is to pronounce upon woman the verdict that she is by nature inclined to sexual change, and this every woman knows is a lie. I hurl the infamous insinuation back in the teeth of whoever dare make it, as a libel upon my sex, based upon the practices of men and not upon the natural instincts of women.

I make the claim boldly, that from the very moment woman is emancipated from the necessity of yielding the control of her sexual organs to man to insure a home, food and clothing, the doom of sexual demoralization will be sealed. From that moment there will be no sexual intercourse except such as is desired by women. It will be a complete revolution in sexual matters, in which men will have to take a back seat and be content to be servants where they have been masters so long. The present system is at variance with everything in nature. Everywhere, except among men and women, the female has supreme authority in the domain of sex, and the male never pretends to oppose it, nor to appeal from its decisions. Compare men and women with the animals and see how far below them they have fallen in this regard. Yet among animals the principle of freedom is thoroughly exemplified. Why are they not degraded, debauched and diseased? Simply because the female is the dominant power in sex. What would be the result among animals were the barbarous rule of marriage enforced ; were the female to be compelled to submit herself without reserve to the lecherous instincts of the male? It would be the same that has obtained among women—disease everywhere, until there is scarcely a sexually healthy woman past the age of puberty to be found. This is the purity, this the morality, this the divinity of marriage. Oh, God! is there no power that can restore woman to the level of the brutes? Is their nothing that can rescue her from this shameless condition, from this pollution, this nastiness?

To woman, by nature, belongs the right of sexual determination. When the instinct is aroused in her, then and then only should commerce follow. When woman rises from sexual slavery into freedom, into the ownership and control of her sexual organs, and man is obliged to respect this freedom, then will this instinct become pure and holy; then will woman be raised from the iniquity and morbidness in which she now wallows for existence, and the intensity and glory of her creative functions be increased a hundred-fold; then may men and women, like the beasts or the birds, if they will, herd together, and the instinct in woman, by the law of natural attraction and adaptation, rouse in man its answering counterpart, and its counterpart only.

This is the purity at which I aim; this is the holiness to which I would have woman and, through her functions, the sexual relations elevated; this is the glory with which I would have woman crowned; this is what it means to be virtuous; this what it means to be pure. Again I ask, is there a man or woman who hears me who will ever dare hereafter to associate this doctrine with the debased and the low, and call it an attempt to descend further into lust and license?

Oh, woman! would that the beautiful, the shining, the redeemed of heaven could come to you in their white-robed purity and sing in your ears the blessed song of the angels who "neither marry nor are given in marriage," and who live in their own natural element of freedom. Oh! that they could come to you as they have to me, and show how, through you, as represented by Eve—through your sexual slavery to men—has sin, and misery and crime been introduced into the world; and how through the assertion and maintenance of your sexual freedom and purity only, can "the seed of the woman bruise the serpent's head," and humanity be restored to its original sexual purity, the Scripture fulfilled and the millennium ushered in.

Instead of opposing this doctrine, the Churches should see that through its propagation only can their sacred prophecies be realized. Instead of denouncing me the ministers ought to be my most earnest advocates, not merely because through the theory of Free Love only can their lives be justified, but because by its practice alone can salvation come to the world. They have been working at the wrong end of salvation; they have been trying to save souls while their bodies were damned. Now let them save bodies, and the souls will take care of themselves. I should be glad to believe that these clerical persons are honest, but I cannot. They know the sad lives of thousands of women, suffering and yearning for comfort and sympathy; these women go to their pastors for relief, and I have the very best of reasons for believing, indeed, I know that in numerous instances, they not only get that for which they yearn, but also that further comfort and sympathy to which the others naturally lead, and which the ministers know they can so safely administer. This is another reason to be added to the matter of fees, which I have already mentioned, why this class do not wish the marriage relations disturbed. The ministers, lawyers and doctors have a monopoly of this field, and they intend to keep it.

The world will have a genuine surprise some day when it shall awaken to the truth, as I know it, about the churches; to a knowledge of the kind of currency in which lawyers often receive their divorce fees. As this, however, is none of my business, I shall let the world take its own time about it. But I sometimes think it would be only a just reward for their stupidity were husbands to be shown why it is that their wives are so earnest in religious matters. Everybody knows that the churches would totter and tumble if it were not for the women. Men have mostly grown out of churches, and attend them because their families wish it, so that the "pew rent" may be paid. There are many churches besides Plymouth in which half the women are in love with their pastors; and in these cases I think it safe to say, as it is in that of Plymouth, it is usually reciprocated.

But as to the difficulty of freedom for woman : There is but one, and that is pecuniary independence. I know that opposers refer to the condition of women in Greece and Rome, when there were few restrictions sexually, and use it as an argument against freedom now. But it doesn't apply, and I will show you why. In those times it mattered not whether there were marriage laws or not. In either case woman was dependent upon her sex for support; if married, then upon her husband ; if not married, then upon her lover.

So the mere abolition of marriage does not necessarily mean sexual freedom for woman. I do not hesitate to admit that marriage has played its necessary part in the evolution of society; nor that among a people where women have a very limited position in the industrial organization, that it provides them a support. I will go so far even as to say that, so long as women prefer to depend upon the sale of their sexual favors rather than upon their industrial capacities for support, that marriage may be deemed a sort of protection. But I also hold that, to a woman who prefers rather to rely upon her own talent for support, marriage is intolerable.

This is the same argument that was used by the slaveholders. "Slaves," they said, "were better off as slaves than they could be, free. They need to be taken care of; and until they are capable of self-support it is best that slavery continue." The slaves themselves generally coincided with this idea. Only a few of the more intelligent saw that the argument was a deceit.

So now do most women coincide with the same argument as applied to marriage. Only a few who have solved the question for themselves, see that it is fallacious. In spite of the argument the anti-slavery revolution came, and violently cast the slaves upon their own resources. Who is there who now dare say their condition is not improved? So will it be with women. They will hesitate to take the responsibility of freedom. They will say: "I prefer to rely upon my sex a little longer." But the revolution will come eventually, and thrust them upon their own resources; and in ten years nobody will be found to doubt that their condition has been improved.

But the old argument as applied to women is fallacious in still another way, as I will show. Suppose that all the women in the land, on a given day, should rise and throw off the yoke of marriage, and declare and hold themselves free, how long would it be before the men would accede to any terms? Do you think it would be a month—three weeks—two weeks? I haven't the slightest idea that they would hold out a single week. Women are entirely unaware of their power. Like an elephant led by a string, they are subordinated by a writing, drawn up by just those who are most interested in holding them in slavery. I am sometimes almost out of patience at the servility with which women fawn upon their masters, when they might lead them by the nose wherever they please.

It is sometimes asked: "If what you say is true, and that marriage is a curse, why did not the deprecated results obtain years ago?" I will show you why. It will be remembered that it used to be said by the slaveholders, that the moment a slave got the freedom crotchet into his head he was no longer of any account. A negro was a good slave so long as the idea of freedom was not born in his soul. Whenever this birth occurred he began to feel the galling of his chains.

It is the same with women. So long as they entertain the idea that their natural destiny is to be owned and cared for by some man, whom they are to repay by the surrender of their person, they are good, legal wives; but from the moment the notion that they have an individual right to themselves—to the control of their bodies and maternal functions—has birth in their souls, they become bad wives. They rebel in their souls, if not in words and deeds; and the legal claims of their husbands become a constant source of annoyance, and the enforcement of their legal rights an unbearable thing.

It is this repugnance, this sexual rebellion, that is causing the degradation and widespread disease among women, sexually; and this reacts upon man, and degrades him. The mind, in rebellion at the enslaved condition, has such an effect upon the sexual act that it becomes impossible for its subject to respond or reciprocate; and the organs suffer the natural penalty.

In speaking of this almost anomalous condition in woman, Dr. John M. Scudder, Professor of the Diseases of Women in the Cincinnati Medical College, says: "If the act is complete, so that both body and mind are satisfied, no disease arises, though there be frequent repetitions; but if the act be incomplete, the organs being irritated merely, and the mind not satisfied, then disease will surely follow. There is no doubt that the proper gratification of the function is conducive to health and longevity; or that its abuse leads to disease and shortens life. Therefore," he adds, "the wife should not lose control of her person in marriage. It is hers to rule supreme in this regard. This is a law of life, and is violated in no species except in man."

What better confirmation could there be of all that I have been trying to enforce upon you, than these words from this large-hearted man and widely-experienced physician? Every wife should obtain the book from which I quote these words, and study it carefully. It is entitled, "The Reproductive Organs," and has just been published by Wilstach, Baldwin & Co., of Cincinnati, Ohio.

I said at the outset that I am endeavoring to effect a revolution in marriage, or rather to replace the institution by a better method of providing for women as mothers and children as progeny. Everybody admits that our social system is far from perfect. Society, like everything else in the universe, evolves by natural laws. Marriage is not the perfect condition. It will be replaced by another and more perfect, which will be a legitimate outcome of the old. As republicanism in politics is a legitimate child of constitutional monarchy, so in socialism shall personal freedom be the offspring of legal limitation; and when it shall come, not anybody will doubt its parentage or question its legitimacy.

Sexual freedom, then, means the abolition of prostitution both in and out of marriage; means the emancipation of woman from sexual slavery and her coming into ownership and control of her own body; means the end of her pecuniary dependence upon man, so that she may never even seemingly, have to procure whatever she may desire or need by sexual favors; means the abrogation of forced pregnancy, of ante-natal murder, of undesired children; means the birth of love-children only, endowed by every inherited virtue that the highest exaltation can confer at conception, by every influence for good to be obtained during gestation, and by the wisest guidance and instruction on to manhood, industrially, intellectually and sexually.

It means no more sickness, no more poverty, no more crime: it means peace, plenty and security, health, purity and virtue; it means the replacement of money-getting as the aim of life by the desire to do good; the closing of hospitals and asylums, and the transformation of prisons, jails and penitentiaries into workshops and scientific schools; and of lawyers, doctors and ministers into industrial artizans; it means equality, fraternity and justice raised from the existence which they now have in name only, into practical life; it means individual happiness, national prosperity and universal good.

Ultimately, it means more than this even. It means the establishment of co-operative homes, in which thousands who now suffer in every sense shall enjoy all the comforts and luxuries of life, in the place of the isolated households which have no care for the misery and destitution of their neighbors. It means for our cities, the conversion of innumerable huts into immense hotels, as residences; and the combination of all industrial enterprises upon the same plan; and for the country, the co-operative conduct of agriculture by the maximum of improvements for labor-saving, and the consequent reduction of muscular toil to the minimum. And it means the inter-co-operation of all these in a grand industrial organization to take the places of the present governments of the world, whose social basis shall be all people united in the great human family as brothers and sisters.

So after all I am a very promiscuous Free Lover. I want the love of you all, promiscuously. It makes no difference who or what you are, old or young, black or white, Pagan, Jew, or Christian, I want to love you all and be loved by you all; and I mean to have your love. If you will not give it to me now, these young, for whom I plead, will in after years bless Victoria Woodhull for daring to speak for their salvation. It requires a strong and a pure woman to go before the world and attack its most cherished institution. No one who has not passed through the fiery furnace of affliction, and been purged of selfishness by the stern hand of adversity, and become emancipated from public opinion, could stand the load of opprobium that I have been forced to carry. I sometimes grow weary under its weight and sigh for rest, but my duty to my sex, spurs me on. Therefore I want your sympathy, your sustaining love, to go with me and bless me; and when I leave you for other fields of labor and stand upon other rostrums, fearing I may not be able to do my duty, I want to feel the yearnings of your hearts following me with prayers that my efforts may be blessed. I want the blessings of these fathers, the affections of these sons, the benedictions of these mothers and the prayers of these daughters to follow me everywhere, to give me strength to endure the labor, courage to speak the truth and a continued faith that the right will triumph.

And may the guardian angels who are hovering over you carry the benign light of freedom home to your souls to bless each sorrowing heart, to relieve each suffering body, and to comfort each distressed spirit as it hath need, is the blessing which I leave with you.

www.ingramcontent.com/pod-product-compliance
Lightning Source LLC
LaVergne TN
LVHW011231080426
835509LV00005B/438